THESE .
A Life ᴏ̤ ᴛʜᴏᴍas Paine

Thomas Paine

THESE ARE THE TIMES

A Life of Thomas Paine

An original screenplay by
Trevor Griffiths

Geoff .
Good wishes
Trevor Griffiths

SPOKESMAN

First published in 2005 by Spokesman
Russell House, Bulwell Lane
Nottingham
NG6 0BT
Phone 0115 970 8318.   Fax 0115 942 0433
e-mail elfeuro@compuserve.com
www.spokesmanbooks.com

ISBN 0 85124 695 8

A CIP catalogue is available from the British Library

Printed by the Russell Press Ltd (phone 0115 978 4505).

For Richard Attenborough
comrade and collaborator on this long march

Second Street. Friday Even'g —

Sir

Two letters of Mr. S. Deane's having appeared in the N. Y papers which are variously commented upon, I should like to converse a quarter of an hour with you on that subject. — I hope this Man's knack of creating confusion and involving characters in suspicion is at an end. — Whether the letters be genuine or not I do not undertake to give judgment upon, but his language in France is equally as strange as any thing contained in these publications.

I am Sir
your Obt. Hble Servt.
Thomas Paine

Hon'ble R. Morris Esquire

Thomas Paine's letter to Robert Morris, 2nd November 1781 (as used on cover).

Trevor Griffiths

Trevor Griffiths was born in Manchester in 1935, of Irish and Welsh descent. He read English at Manchester University and worked as a teacher, a liberal studies lecturer and a further education officer for the BBC before becoming a full-time writer in 1970. During the late 1950s and early 1960s, he edited a series of publications for the Workers' Northern Publishing Society, including *Labour's Northern Voice.*

He has been writing for the theatre, television and cinema since the late 1960s. His work has been seen throughout the world and has won numerous awards. His best known stage play, *Comedians*, has been in constant production around the world since its première in 1975. Among his many other stage plays are *Thatcher's Children, Piano* and *The Gulf Between Us,* which was written in the year following the first Iraq War and which he directed himself. It opened at the West Yorkshire Playhouse in 1992 on the anniversary of the beginning of the war.

For his film *Reds*, written with Warren Beatty, he received the Writers Guild of America Best Screenplay award and an Oscar nomination. Other films have included *Country* directed by Richard Eyre and *Fatherland* directed by Ken Loach. In 1982 he won the BAFTA Writers Award.

He is known both for his original works – contemporary and historical – and for his adaptations of works by writers such as Lawrence and Chekhov, including *The Cherry Orchard* and a seven-part adaptation of *Sons and Lovers.* In the mid 1970s, he wrote the celebrated eleven-part television series *Bill Brand* about a young left-wing Labour MP struggling to radicalise his increasingly right-wing party. He also wrote the television film series *The Last Place on Earth,* about the race for the South Pole between Scott and Amundsen.

From the 1980s onwards he has also directed his own work both in theatre and on film. *Food for Ravens*, which he both wrote and directed, is a poetic re-imagining of the life and death of Aneurin Bevan and won both a Royal Television Society award and the first Gwyn A Williams Award at the Welsh Baftas in 1998. In the mid-1990s he wrote and directed the stage play *Who Shall be Happy...?*, about the French Revolution and the death of Danton, which was also produced for television under the title *Hope in the Year Two*.

Work in progress includes a stage play about the Lancashire comedian Frank Randle, a new stage play for the Royal Shakespeare Company, and a film project based on the book *A Short Walk in the Hindu Kush*.

A complete list of Trevor Griffiths' work can be found on his website at www.TrevorGriffiths.co.uk.

Foreword

'The most ambitious of Griffiths' projects during this time [the 1980s/1990s] is surely his screenplay on the life of Tom Paine, the first draft of which occupied him during much of 1988-89. Griffiths was first approached with the idea by director Sir Richard Attenborough, who phoned him in early 1987 while he was in South Wales working on the Miners' Strike project. Griffiths spent 1988 researching and writing the script, eventually completing a first draft titled *These Are the Times* in January 1989. After a number of meetings with Attenborough, Griffiths completed a second draft that June and a revised version of this draft in December. Attenborough has continued to try to line up financing, and though it has appeared at several points on the verge of being launched, the project is still ongoing. Griffiths completed a third draft in January 1995 and a fourth draft in May 1999 and remains hopeful concerning a text that he considers a favourite of his.

These Are the Time is indeed an epic script, equal in scale and ambition to *Reds*. Indeed, Griffiths' screenplay recalls the earlier film in a number of ways, most notably in its parallel narratives of revolution and revolutionary activism: part one deals with Paine's arrival in the American colonies and his participation in the American Revolution, while part two focuses on Paine's experience during the French Revolution. Following *Reds* and *Real Dreams, These Are the Times* can be seen as the continuation of Griffiths' interest in the radical tradition central to American national identity. It also represents a deconstruction, on Griffiths' part, of the largely Anglo-Saxon idea of America that would serve such repressive functions in the nation's subsequent history. Griffiths' portrait of colonial America is a richly multicultural one, a polyphony of different languages and people, including blacks and Iroquois Indians (Paine makes a point of insisting that Indians, too, are Americans.) And, consistent with his practice throughout his career, Griffiths challenges the prevailing myths of the American Revolution and the 'Founding Fathers' by portraying them in terms of conflicting visions and class interests. As *These Are the Times* suggests, the Revolution began writing itself as myth from the very start (Griffiths' Washington is particularly given to self-iconizing).

Against the backdrop of both revolutions Paine stands as a truth seeker, even when this activity conflicts with official versions of reality. Griffiths acknowledges that his portrait of Paine draws very much on his sense of himself as a writer in the late 1980s: 'I think a lot of how I was feeling in the '80s ... goes into that piece.' The connections are particularly evident in the second half as Paine, whose life has been spent negotiating the borders of cultures and worlds (England, America, France), now finds himself out of place in all three countries, insisting on ideals and imperatives in worlds in which they no longer seem to belong. Romantically unattached for most of the years covered by Griffiths' text, he is an increasingly lonely figure as *These Are the Times* progresses, overtaken by age and increasingly an anachronism. Perhaps the most poignant moment comes when Paine, released from his French prison, returns to the United States. He meets his friend Jefferson in the White House banquet room only to discover that, on the wall of portraits commemorating the heroes of the Revolution, his portrait is missing – 'erased from the record', as Griffiths' direction states.

In the conclusion to his March 1983 speech to the National Association of Evangelicals (the famous occasion on which he branded the Soviet Union an 'evil empire'), Ronald Reagan quoted Paine: 'We have it within our power to begin the world over again.' *These Are the Times* is Griffiths' effort to reclaim this vision of rebirth and transformation from the social and political conservatism that has historically appropriated it – to defamiliarize the language of American democracy and reveal the radically liberationist discourse at its heart. In his last official action in France, Paine addresses the National Assembly as it debates the proposed French Constitution. Paine dismisses the document as 'contemptible' and recalls the vision of Jefferson's Declaration of Independence: 'One phrase above all others lit a beacon that burns now in men's hearts everywhere: All men are created equal. All men. Not all gentlemen, not all men of wealth and property and education, not all men of power, privilege, connexion. All.' At the dawn of a modernity that the United States will eventually preside over (Griffiths' closing camera shot tilts from the site of Paine's New Rochelle grave to reveal a modern highway) the vision that these words embody represents the country's founding dream of human justice and equality.'

Stanton B. Garner Jr.,
from Trevor Griffiths: Politics, Drama, History
The University of Michigan Press, 1999

"These are the times that try men's souls. The summer soldier and the sunshine patriot will, in this crisis, shrink from the service of their country, but he that stands it now deserves the love and thanks of man and woman ... It matters not where you live, or what rank of life ye hold, the evil or the blessing will reach you all. The far and the near, the home counties and the back, the rich and the poor, will suffer or rejoice alike ..."

The American Crisis No. 1

"The sun never shone on a cause of greater worth ... Tis not the affair of a city, a country, a province, or a kingdom, but of a continent – of at least one-eighth part of the habitable globe. Tis not the concern of a day, a year or an age; posterity are virtually involved in the contest, and will be more or less affected even to the end of time, by the proceedings now ... O ye that love mankind, ye that dare oppose not only the tyranny but the tyrant, stand forth to receive the fugitive and prepare in time an asylum for humanity ..."

Common Sense on Independence

THESE ARE THE TIMES

PHILADELPHIA, 1787 An old man's voice, singing snatches of "The World Turned Upside Down".

OLD MAN'S VOICE: "... If summer were spring and the other way round, Then all the World would be upside down ..."

The song stops, kicks abruptly into speech.

OLD MAN'S VOICE: ... It grieves me we chose the bald eagle for our national symbol ...

Wharf Street, *vivid with life. Two men leg a sedan chair through the crowd.*

OLD MAN'S VOICE: ... he's a bird of bad moral character, generally poor and often very lousy ...

The camera gradually closes on the sedan,

OLD MAN'S VOICE: ... The turkey's our own stock and a much more respectable creature ...

reveals eventually the shadowy occupant, a bald old man of eighty, imp's eyes in plump face. He stares from the window gap, as if at the lens.

OLD MAN: Never mind ... Twenty years back there was no America, just a baker's dozen of seaboard colonies fretting at Mother England's apron strings and skriking for first turn at the tit ...

The old man stares vaguely through window. He turns his head deliberately, eyes the lens.

OLD MAN: Thirteen colonies, thirteen clocks. By what miracle did they come to strike all at the same time, mm? Taxes, was it? On calico, on newspapers, on tea ...?

We see the padded fabric inner wall of the chair, empty save for his ragged wig dancing from a peg.

OLD MAN'S VOICE: ... Georgia made its own calico, Delaware barely had newspapers and didn't give a damn for 'em, Virginia drank coffee ...

His hand reaches into the shot, removes the wig. He places it floppily on his ample head. Glances out through the window.

OLD MAN: When the world changes, it's **people** do the changing, masses of 'em. And when a people becomes a nation, as we did, throws not just tea but a king, parliament and a whole history of dependence overboard, ye can be sure it's not just a famous handful involved in the doing, your Washingtons, your Jeffersons, your Adamses ... *(An impish smile)* ... your Franklins, if ye'll pardon the presumption. Nameless, unnumberable, unlettered, unrecorded and unremarked, when the mongrel folk decided government was too important to leave to their betters, they upped and calmly reinvented the future, not just their own but the world's ...

A commotion outside brings the chair to a halt: grunts, shouts, expostulation. The old man puts his head out to see, a great black hog rears up from the ruck to snap at him, he snouts it briskly with his cane, the chair moves on.

OLD MAN: As a matter o' fact, it was no miracle brought the thirteen clocks to strike all together back there ... It was Common Sense, 'least that's what he called himself ... Tom Pain he was when I met him, Tom nobody from nowhere, I was unofficial ambassador for Philadelphia in London, he came to ask me about the new world, just another of the nameless unnumberables looking for the future ...

The chair stops. He looks out. Sees someone. Waves his stick at him.

OLD MAN: I loaned him the passage out. A good day's work. See for yourself.

He points the stick down the wharf. We see, as if in his point of view

LONDON, *September 1774, A long fog-smeared wharf,* *berthing a navy frigate one end, an Atlantic packet at the other. A slow pulse of people arriving, assembling, seeking direction. Pain heads steadily through the confusion, bags in hand.*

From ahead, sounds of coarse laughter, horseplay,
raucous, drink-tinged.

We move into a tavern, heavy with the din of Redcoats
drinking up before shipping out. NCOs move about the
place, trying to keep order. Pain arrives from the street,
scans the room a moment, carries his meagre baggage to
the bar, orders rum, surveys the bedlam as he waits. He's
tall, mid-thirties, strong-bodied; eyes calm and still inside
the moil of the room. NCOs chivvy the squaddies to drink
up and muster outside for the boat for Boston. A patriotic
song sets up, other tables join in, a large Scots sergeant
climbs onto a bench by the fire to toast the King and get
the men on their feet. Pain's rum arrives as the room
quietens for the loyal address. He pays his halfpenny.
Listens a moment.

SERGEANT: Raise jugs for the loyal toast, laddies! To our
    gracious sovereign King George, in whose service we
    sail for Boston to restore law and loyalty among his
    misguided colonial subjects ...

Pain sinks the rum. Shoulders his bags. Leaves, mid-toast.
He stands a while beneath the tavern's gaudy King's Head
sign, watching drunken soldiery being mustered and
marched towards the waiting troopship for Boston, orders
barking across the dank air. A bought crowd waves its
bought royal favours with bought enthusiasm. Squads of
Hessian merceneries in their strange hunting-green
uniforms answer roll-call on the dockside, adding
German to the din. Pain heads away, picks a path through
the growing turmoil, past carriages and carts decanting
officers, troops and camp-followers onto the quay, round
clusters of blind and maimed war-veterans begging
another day's supplies, towards the quiet file of
passengers boarding the second ship, the Packet for
Philadelphia. From the deck, as the line moves upwards,
the passenger roll-call is already under way. The man in
front hears his name called.

MAN: *(Yells)* O'Connell, here, sir!.

He shares a smile with Pain just below. O'Connell's pregnant wife touches her husband's hand gently. Pain looks on.

The deck, *shrouded in fog, alive with Europe's poor shipping out for service in the New World: Germans, Dutch, Scots, Gaels, Welsh, English. A ship's officer does his best with their names: voices rise in answer from the crowded deck.*

Pain stands by the rail, on the edge of things.

Voices lift from the murk below. He looks down to the quayside. Two young Guards officers press tipsy farewells on an elegantly pissed young blood about to climb aboard. Behind their fine carriage, a small cart draws up, laden with his baggage. A boy servant begins unloading. A young woman climbs down with him from the cart, gathers her own scant things. The young blood ignores them, bids a last farewell, heads up the gangway. Servant and young woman toil after him. Half-way up, the young woman lifts her eyes, catches Pain's stare. She's very young, slight, sharply rouged, in her poor travelling best.

SHIP'S OFFICER: ... Thomas Pain.

Pain looks back at the deck, calls "Aye".

The ship's officer ticks his sheet, presses doggedly on, nearing completion. A bell sounds somewhere, the ship's captain appears on an upper deck, a bible in his hand.

YOUNG BLOOD: John Anderson, if you please, there ...

The ship's officer looks up from his roll, checks for the entry, finds it on page one.

SHIP'S OFFICER: Welcome aboard, Captain Anderson. Your quarters await you, sir ...

Anderson swings his cane forward inquiringly, the officer nods, the man walks off. Pain watches the laden boy stagger after him, the young woman in his wake. The bell sounds again, the deck stills, the ship's captain opens his bible.

4

SHIP'S CAPTAIN: *(Dry, Scots)* The Lord reigneth; let the earth rejoice. Make a joyful noise unto the Lord, all ye lands. Know ye that the Lord He is God; it is He that hath made us, and not we ourselves; we are His people. *(Closes book)* Let us pray for the good Lord's protection and a safe passage upon His uncertain seas ... *(Prays)* ... Our Father, which art in Heaven ...

Language by language, the deck joins the captain's paternoster. We see the O'Connells, others, deep in the prayer. Pain looks on, at the edge, lips still; as with the Loyal Toast, not part of what he watches.

The ship's deck. *Night. Mist; a moon somewhere; calm. In the crow's nest, strapped to the forward mast, a boy scans for ice. Below deck, low voices sing a hymn in German.*

Pain appears from below, a bucket in each hand, fills them from a rain barrel by the deckhouse. A woman, cloaked and hatted, her back to him, stands at the rail, staring into the mist. He dwells a moment, unsure why; uneasy. She turns suddenly to look at him, her face barely visible in the gloom; it's Captain Anderson's young companion. Pain nods. She turns abruptly away.

Steerage. *Pain, buckets in hands, threads a passage through the two hundred or so indentured underclass packed into the low-beamed 'tween-decks like clothing. He lays one bucket down by a grateful German tending several sick children; carries the second on to a group of sick Irish. O'Connell thanks him with a scared smile, resumes sponging his fevered wife. Her eyes open briefly, see nothing. Trails of disjointed prayer lift and die on her cracked lips.*

Pain stands, scans the hell-hole. The sick are already everywhere. The Germans end their hymn. The Welsh start up another.

The passageway to the cabins. *Pain swings an oil-lamp to light the way. Pauses a moment by a large oak door. Men's drunken laughter, travelling gentry at play: Pain reads **John Anderson, Esq. Bt**. scrolled up on the wood. A boy squeals, in pain; more laughter.*

5

The lamp swings, in movement again, the passageway danker, less ornate. The light catches something ahead. Pain's face as he stoops over the prone young woman, curled up under her cloak, face to wall, eyes open.

PAIN: Are you sick? *(She shakes her head)* Do you need help?

WOMAN: *(Toneless; Southwark cockney)* Help? Not from no **man**, I don't.

He leans forward a touch, lamp up, studies the thick bruising about her cheek and temple.

PAIN: Was it a man gave you that?

She raises a hand to shield the damage. Pain stares at the contused and swollen fingers. Stands.

PAIN: The face may heal itself, the hand will take helping ... Will I do it?

A movement catches his eye: down the passage, the tiny boy servant stares at him fearfully.

Pain's cabin. *His hand turns up a slung oil-lamp. Light trembles across the meagre space. When he turns to close the door, he sees the young woman has followed him.*

YOUNG WOMAN: You'll want paying ...

He shakes his head, beckons her to sit at the make-shift desk, closes the door behind her, adjusts the lamp to examine the damaged face and hands. She takes in the rudimentary room, the scant possessions, the pair of globes, three books, paper, ink and pen on the desk; gasps occasionally, as he feels the hand.

PAIN: I'll need your stays.

She blinks. He reaches for a workman's leather pouch, takes out a knife, some fine twine, a length of coarse wadding; she removes her corset. He begins to work the whalebones loose with the blade. She looks on, drawn. Looks at the books again, (Newton's Principia, Franklin's Poor Richard's Almanack, Pilgrim's Progress), the blank writing paper.

YOUNG WOMAN: What are you? Are you a surgeon? Or a scribbler, is it?

PAIN: *(Absorbed in work)* I'm a staymaker. *(He looks up, smiles, the blue eyes gentling)* Here ...

He reaches forward, places the wadding in her bruised mouth, uncorks a bottle of rum, pours a full cup. Takes the battered hand with delicate care. Snaps the dislocated index finger back into its socket.

WOMAN: *(All she can manage)* Shooshus!

He removes the wadding, hands her the rum. She swigs, face pale with pain. He lays the hand on the desk, builds a four-bone splint around the wadding with the twine.

PAIN: And what are you?

WOMAN: Me? I'm a whore.

He looks up at her for a moment; nods; returns to the splint.

YOUNG WOMAN: Philly, my mother says, a cunt'll allus 'ave a market while fuckin' remains the custom in Europe ... I don't expect America'll prove her a liar. I travel at the convenience of Captain John Bully Anderson, he pays my passage ... That's the world.

PAIN: *(Finishing up)* No, no. That's just the world we have. *(He raises the lamp again to see her face.)* My God, you're but a child. You could be my daughter.

A knock at the door; the boy servant calls her name, tells her the master wants her. Philly stands. Collects her purse. Crosses to leave.

PHILLY: I thank you.

She raises the splinted hand; means more. Pain nods. She's gone. He sits for a moment; spots she's left her stays on the desk; picks them up. Beneath them, in close up, the virgin paper. A bead of liquid splashes onto the surface; another. Pain's face staring down, cobbed with sweat.

7

Day. The ship, inching past a vast dwarfing iceberg. The screen begins to fill with white.

Close shot as a dozen or so hessian-wrapped dead are prayerfully despatched over the side.

Cabin. Pain's face on his pillow. Fever rages. His eyes open, close; his lips reach soundlessly for meanings beyond him.

The ship again, the iceberg towering above it. A woman screams, in dreadful pain.

Cabin. Pain, back arched, in fevered convulsion. Philly's hands, one of them still splinted, come in to push him down again. Pain's fevered face on the pillow, eyes open, seeing nothing.

Night. Full profile shot of the ship again, as before, inching past the unending ice. Very slowly, land and sky begin to show beyond, as the ship passes the berg. The sky is lightening: sunrise. The screen fades to black.

PHILADELPHIA, 1774, Dockside. A hard, bright November morning. The London Packet has all but emptied. People clog the cobbled quays, some on their knees giving thanks. Carts and wagons fringe the crowd; back-country farmers mustering their newly-arrived bond servants. Din, hustle, energy: America's largest port and only city.

Anderson, in city clothes now, picks a purposeful path through the mêlée, headed for a waiting carriage. The servant-boy struggles after him, loaded with gear. We watch all this from the shadow of a large draught-horse, where Philly is tucking herself in to make sure Anderson doesn't spot her. Anderson exchanges greetings with two men by the carriage; stares casually around for his whore; then all three climb in; leave. Philly gives the cartman a copper coin, beckons him to follow, plunges off into the moil. She scans faces, pushing on; stoops to look at half a dozen dead laid out on straw, labels pinned to clothing, some with wooden counters on their eyes.

O'Connell and his son, hats in hands, stand by a farmer's cart, already claimed. The boy sees something, tugs his father's sleeve, points towards the ship. We see two seamen stretcher a body and baggage down the gangway on a sailcloth. O'Connell leaves his son with the bags, hurries off towards them. The seamen flip body and baggage onto a bed of clean straw, one gathers the sailcloth, the other rights the prone body, they return to the ship.

A close shot of Pain's face on the straw bed, eyes closed, skin deathly. His eyes blink suddenly open. The sound fades as we move to his point of view of sky, rigging; the occasional curious face peering in and passing on. Ambient sound pulses in, out, unreal, unreliable. O'Connell appears, crouches, his eyes raw, ravaged.

O'CONNELL: God bless you mister ...

He reaches down, overcome now, to squeeze Pain's shoulder.

PAIN: *(A croak)* ... Missus ...?

O'Connell shakes his head once, the tears hot in his nose.

O'CONNELL: ... God's will ...

The sound fades to mute again. Skyline and O'Connell's face blur; fade. The skyline, rigging, up again. Sounds: Philly's voice calling his name, wheels over cobblestone, the clop of a horse. Philly's face pushes into the frame. She smiles.

The screen fades to black.

Mrs Downey's boarding house. *Night. Pain's candlelit face on a pillow, eyes closed. The lips mutter on some old argument. The eyes open abruptly, struggle for focus.*

An African boy, ten maybe, peers uncertainly down at him, the candle in his hand.

PAIN: Who are you? *(Nothing)* Do you understand me? *(The boy frowns; nods)* Where am I?

AFRICAN BOY: Mis' Downey's place. Walnut 'n' Chestnut.

PAIN: Philadelphia?

The African boy frowns again.

BOY: I call missus.

He leaves. His shadow crosses the cracked ceiling. Fade to black.

The same room, daytime now. Pain's face on pillow, eyes open. Somewhere just outside the room a Scots voice is reading a letter:

VOICE: "... The bearer Mr Thomas Pain is well recommended to me as an ingenious worthy young man with some skill at writing. He goes to Pennsylvania with a view of settling there. If you can put him in a way of obtaining employment, perhaps in teaching or instruction, you will do well and much oblige your affectionate father-in-law."

Pain angles his head, finds the shadows of a man and a woman in muttered talk out on the stair-head landing. His lips move to call them; nothing comes. He struggles to upright, edges his feet to the floor, eyes burning, fierce with effort.

MAN: *(Showing her)* And that's from Benjamin Franklin, no less, Mrs Downey.

MRS DOWNEY: The hand of a great man, so it is, Doctor. The young lady gave it me before she left.

Pain shakes water into a wooden beaker; drinks deep, levers himself upright, dizzies, steadies.

DOCTOR: You did well, I'll see it's delivered this evening to Mr Bache.

The pair begin to descend the staircase, talk on a moment as they go: she asks if he might yet die, the doctor worries he might not recover all his faculties.

*Pain inches stiffly towards the window-seat; makes it. Slumps, sucking air. Gathers again, edging his body for a view of the city through the snow-rimmed panes. He watches wide-eyed for some moments, missing nothing. His cracked lips are in movement, framing a meaning. A word arrives there: **Philadelphia**. He blinks, exultant. New sounds bubble up, throat to mouth. He fingers his lips like a blind man reading. Discovers he's laughing.*

***Mr Bache's house.** Day. A hand clacks a large door-knocker. Pain waits, small cow-hide satchel in one hand. Across Front Street, a street-auction has just begun, a pair of chestnut mares under the hammer. Further on, a group of Iroquois use a tree for target-practice. A servant answers the door. Pain asks for Mr Bache, gives his name, steps into the fine gleaming house. Pain waits on, glancing from time to time at his reflection in a large glass cabinet. Men's voices in meeting from a nearby room. The argument grows heated.*

BACHE'S VOICE: *(Impassioned)* Damn Massachusetts, damn Sam Adams and damn his Boston rebels, my life and livelihood depend on trade with Britain, war is out of the question ...

Sarah Bache, Franklin's daughter, appears from the kitchen, a maidservant in tow carrying a tray of food.

MRS BACHE: If you're come to mend the privy, it's at the back, someone should have shown you ...

PAIN: I'm waiting for Mr Bache, ma'am.

MRS BACHE: Indeed? My husband is in meeting, has he been informed?

PAIN: I believe so, ma'am.

MRS BACHE: Well wait by the study there, I'll enquire when he might be free ...

He watches her enter the meeting room, to some applause from the hungry. Crosses to the study, peers in at the room through the open door. The near wall carries several portraits and prints of Franklin. Pain approaches them, drawn, respect in his eyes. The old guy beams down at him.

Bache in, plump, purposeful, important.

BACHE: So. What can I do for you, Mister ...?

PAIN: Pain.

BACHE: Pain.

PAIN: I believe you have a letter from Mr Franklin concerning me ...

BACHE: *(Rummaging file from a desk drawer)* Pain, Pain, Pain, Pain. Ah, yes. *(Scanning it)* You arrived some weeks back, I believe ... Dr Kearsley may have mentioned you were sick. Are you recovered?

PAIN: Quite recovered, thank you.

Bache finishes the letter, replaces it in the fat file. Examines the man before him with magisterial exactitude; takes in the declaratory artisan's costume, from wigless head, through coarse jacket and full trousers, leather satchel, down to buckleless shoes.

BACHE: *(Sniffs)* So. If you would care to wait by the door there, I'll ask Mrs Bache to make a note of your particulars ... though I'm bound to say employment does not grow on trees in these parts.

He smiles self-importantly, heads for the door. Pain stands stock-still for some moments, absorbing the rebuff. Sounds of the auction drift in through the window: the barker growing poetic on the dimensions and qualities of the creature under the hammer. Pain slowly approaches the window to get a look. Stops, almost in shock, eyes hardening at the sight: the words used describe not animals but African slaves, roped together on the block.

MRS BACHE: *(From door)* You may wait for me in the **hall**, Mr Pain, while I fetch my daybook ...

He returns to the hallway. She mutters in her maidservant's ear to keep an eye on him, heads off up the polished stairs.

12

MRS BACHE: *(Perfunctory, over shoulder)* ... And how do you find America, Mr Pain?

PAIN: *(Slow)* Oh. Pretty good, ma'am. Though not so perfect it could not stand changing ...

She's gone, barely hearing. He stands for a moment. His eyes catch the watching maidservant's. Voices rise in the merchants' room; a voice tops them all.

BACHE: But what do we have if we have not trade with England? I insure shipping, for God's sake. No, no, no.

Pain turns. Quietly leaves. Bring up sounds of crowded coffee house.

The London Coffee House, *mid-evening - the city's largest and most important meeting-place, lively, serious, rarely less than full. In one half, merchants, professionals, speculators and country gentry, wigged, stocked, breeched and buckled, hold a million post-mortems on the day's dealings. In the other, the trousered classes - artisans, skillmen, journeymen - argue the toss over ale and pie. The boundary is fluid, but the lines are clearly drawn.*

Pain sits alone at a table somewhere between the two, pen in hand, ink out, filling paper with fluent and furious intensity. Page follows page onto the flat leather satchel; the room could be empty, for all he sees or hears of it. A potboy approaches, clearing tables. Silently removes three empty tumblers from Pain's, unnoticed. Watches for a moment. Pain stops abruptly, aware of him now; returns little by little to the crowded room, the rush within him over.

POTBOY: Another glass is it, sir?

PAIN: If you will. Wait though ... *(He fiddles in his pocket for coins; empties three pennies onto the hickory)* Better not ...

The potboy leaves. Pain sits back, frowns briefly at a small white envelope uncovered in the search for cash, returns it to the jacket pockets along with the rest of the

*junk he's accreted, begins gathering and pouching his
things for off. Is drawn by a commotion down the room,
where a skunk has wandered in and settled bewilderedly
in the middle of the coffee house A gang of mechanics
have managed to scare it towards the merchants' end, a
merchant has set his dog on it, the dog has been sprayed
for its trouble and now runs amok amid the Merchants'
tables. People scatter, the mechanics hoot their victory.
Pain chuckles at the madhouse, takes his satchel, leaves
for the street by a door marked "**Necessary**".*

*He clears the building, headed for an alleyway, following
signs to the Necessary House. Just ahead, a group of rich
merchants alight from their carriages to enter the Coffee
House. Several follow him down the alley to the wooden
lean-to. Their talk is loud, contentious, a touch liquored-up.*

*The merchants join Pain at the wooden trough, bringing
their argument with them. Pain is barely noticed.*

BACHE: ... My dear Robert, we cannot **afford** a war, we
   cannot **conduct** a war, and by God there is not one
   possibility in ten thousand we could **win** a war ... Not
   against the British. You really must not believe all you
   read in those damned Boston papers, sir.

*Robert Morris, in fine beaver topcoat, next to Pain,
chuckles deeply, enjoying himself. Pain glances up the
line of faces; spots Bache at the other end, watching him.
Pain holds the stare: no quarter.The others fall silent,
aware of something on.*

BACHE: Pain, isn't it?

PAIN: It is.

BACHE: I believe you owe my wife an apology, sir.

PAIN: I'm most sorry to hear it.

BACHE: Manners maketh man, Mr Pain. He will not rise
   who does not know it.

PAIN: I will bear that in mind. *(He's finished. The rest piss
   on)* Though if it turn me into a patronizing and

overweening creature such as yourself, Mr Bache, I will tell you plainly I would as soon suck shit through a stocking, sir.

He flicks his hat with stiffened finger, walks off into the night. The men stand in silence for some moments.

ROBERT MORRIS: Well, if there **is** to be war with England, gentlemen, I want that man on my side ...

His chuckles release the others into laughter. Bache fumes on.

Mrs Downey's boarding house, *night. Pain stands at the table, just returned, laying out the manuscripts from his satchel in neat piles, removing his coat, preparing to work. He picks up a slip of paper, studies it, crosses to the landing.*

PAIN: Mrs Downey, are you there?

MRS DOWNEY: *(Appearing, foot of stairs)* What is it? I'm serving ...

PAIN: *(Heading down stairs)* What's this?

MRS DOWNEY: *(Occupied)* It's your bill. You asked for it only this morning.

PAIN: ... Mrs Downey, I have been with you five weeks, you have charged but the last two ...

MRS DOWNEY: *(Returning to bar)* ... The others are paid in full, go to your bed. The young lady gave me money 'fore she left ...

PAIN: What young lady?

MRS DOWNEY: Your **daughter**, man. Is it fuddled you are or what? A man does not remember his own daughter, 'n' she a pearl without price ...? Away, away.

She's gone. Pain stands a moment, searching for meaning; finds none.

Pain's room. *Night. A clock strikes two. Four essay-size manuscripts laid out and clipped on the desk; a packet, ready to house them; pen; ink; a poster for The*

Pennsylvania Magazine No.1, a request for essays and articles ringed in ink near the bottom.

Pain lies on the bed, watching roaches on the ceiling. He's still working on the bill, the daughter.

He crosses to a cupboard for his tobacco. Searches pockets. Comes out with pouch and the white envelope. Carries them to the bed. Lights a pipe. Opens the envelope. Takes out a sheet of paper. Holds it close to the candle. Begins to read.

PHILLY'S VOICE: " good buy mr pain yur sickniss ave cost me two weaks but no mater you are a good man and heeled my hand god bless you from philly ps ave fixt for mrs downis africun to see over you til up."

***The Grain Dock**, early morning. Pain works with a small gang of day-labourers, unloading, bagging and carting grain from a small boat. It's a cold, bone-hard day; he sweats under a gun-metal sky. Several merchants watch the work from the quay above, call instructions to the foreman, who answers with respect, cap in hand.*

Pain wipes his forehead; sees Mrs Downey's African boy at the dock-steps, waving at him. Pain leaves the gang, approaches the step. The boy holds a note in his hand; Pain takes it, casts an eye over it. Looks up at the boy.

PAIN: What d'they call ye?

BOY: Will.

Pain nods; winks.

***The street outside Aitken's bookstore**; evening. Watchmen light street-lamps. Pain rattles the door, peers through the glass at the darkened store. A poster announces the first issue of the new Pennsylvania Magazine within; a couple of notices: Assistant wanted, apply within; and Lost, Brown Cow, one black tit, small reward. A man appears from the lit printroom at the rear, glimpsed through an open arch; he carries a lamp in one hand, a large stick in the other; glares through the door pane at him.*

PAIN: Mr Aitken? Thomas Pain, ye asked me to call ...

AITKEN: *(50's; Scots, prickly, old pro)* Are you Pain?

PAIN: I am.

AITKEN: Wait. *(He lays stick and lamp down, begins opening door: two locks, three bolts and a bar.)* Come in. Thought you might be a burglar, this part's plagued by the buggers. *(Begins relocking the door)* Whole country's goin' to pot, ye could spend a week in these parts and niver find an honest man. Come through.

Pain follows him towards a back office behind the counter, pauses to watch the printroom still at work, takes the offered chair before the desk. Aitken's fiddling out Pain's manuscripts, riffling through them; hangs his jacket on a nail, half-obscuring a poster soliciting manuscripts for the new magazine.

AITKEN: Aye. These're no' bad. Might even take one. Ah pay three'n'sixpence apiece, ah don't bargain ... *(Squints at Pain above his specs. Pain nods)* ... That do ye?

PAIN: Aye. Which one d'ye want?

AITKEN: **Might**, ah said. I'm not decided, I'll let ye know. Ye've recently arrived? *(Pain nods)* Word is ye're an awkward beggar, set a flea in old Bache's ear, they say ... *(Pain says nothing)* Are ye in work?

PAIN: Not yet.

AITKEN: Mm. What trade have ye?

PAIN: My trade don't interest me.

AITKEN: Oh? What does?

PAIN: *(Indicating his manuscripts)* This.

AITKEN: Put it out of your head, man. There's no living in letters. *(Silence. He pushes the manuscripts under the lamp again, flicks through them. Sniffs.)* I can't take more than one of these ... *(He fingers seven silver half-joes from his purse, passes them across the table. Pain frowns. Collects them.)* I shall need to keep the others by me a while longer, see how things go ...

PAIN: Ahunh. *(Abruptly, indicating the store)* Have you found your assistant yet? *(Aitken squints at him)* I saw the notice earlier.

AITKEN: Ah've had a couple of enquiries. Why?

PAIN: I might be interested. What does it pay?

AITKEN: Twenty pounds *(He waits.)* 'N' that's more than it's worth.

PAIN: And who is it edits the new magazine?

AITKEN: I do. Hey, hold the holly there ...

PAIN: ... Which is why you need more help in the store, would I be right?

AITKEN: ... Wait on, mister ...

PAIN: ... But there's not enough work in the store, which is why you're only prepared to pay scratchings ...

AITKEN: Scratchings? Listen to me a moment ...

PAIN: ... The right man could do 'em both and still have time for a nap most afternoons ...

AITKEN: ... The right man being one Thomas Pain, I presume ...

PAIN: ... It's possible. I'd need to think on it.

AITKEN: *(Off balance)* Oh you would? I might need to do some thinking of my own, let me tell ye ...

PAIN: How many do ye sell?

AITKEN: Upwards of six hundred, why?

PAIN: *(Deliberately)* If I could not double that by the spring, Mr Aitken, I wouldn't deserve the fifty pounds I'd be asking.

AITKEN: **Fifty**?

PAIN: Of course, I'd ask a free hand as well.

AITKEN: *(Bigger)* **Fifty**??

PAIN: Well, fiftyish. But I'll need to think on it. *(He stands, gathers his things)* I'm much obliged for your time, sir.

AITKEN: Mr Pain. It comes to me upon reasonable authority that you are a staymaker from Norfolk, with not a word published, with not a jot of pertinent experience and, as far as writing goes, not a tittle of training. Am I right?

Pain stares at him across the lamp, his blue unsmiling eyes deadly with life.

PAIN: Mister Aitken, I come to you newborn, much as I came into the world. Into which I dropped, need I remind you, lacking all experience in eating and wholly untrained to breathe. And somehow managed. Your servant, sir.

He leaves. Sees himself out onto the sidewalk. Takes a deep breath. Lets out an amazed, hopeful yell.

PAIN: Philadelphia!

People stop to watch him.

Aiken hears it dimly, still at his desk. Swings round to gather his jacket from the wall-peg. The poster soliciting essays for the new magazine stands revealed. The fee offered, bold type, is 4s.6d. Aitken chuckles.

Early morning. *Will stands outside Mrs Downey's boarding house, the globes in his hands, watching Pain bid farewell to the landlady. Over this we hear Pain's writing voice:*

PAIN VOICE: ... To Americans: That some desperate wretches should be willing to steal and enslave men by violence and murder for gain, is rather lamentable than strange. But that many civilized, nay, Christianised people should approve, and be concerned in the savage practice, is surprising ...

Man and boy walk through hard-rut streets, loaded with gear; flatten themselves for safety against a lean-to, as a maraud of wild black hogs surge by.

PAIN'S VOICE: ... Our traders in men must know the wickedness of that Slave Trade, if they attend to reasoning, or the dictates of their own hearts; and such as shun and stifle all these wilfully sacrifice conscience and the character of integrity to that golden idol ...

They thread through a crowded market area, a multi-lingual boister of blue bonnet Scots, deep-bearded Amish, blackgarbed Mennonites, loud-theeing Quakers, Iroquois braves, fiddling Gaels. A cartload of Redcoats makes its way back to barracks, patrol over, largely ignored by the busy crowd.

PAIN'S VOICE: ... If the slavery of the parents be unjust, much more is their children's ...

Aitken's print-shop. *Pain leads Will up a short flight of steps to a pair of stock-rooms on a half-floor above the shop. Lays down his belongings. Sweeps a table clear for the globes. Gives Will a silver half-joe. Will frowns, shakes his head: it's too much. Pain nods. Will bites it, still unsure. Pain takes a swing at him, the kid scarpers.*

Pain watches the boy out of the printroom. At the doorway he turns, black boy on pale day, to wave. Pain waves back. His writing voice:

... Children are born free; for this is the natural, perfect right of all mankind ...

Pain turns back into his appropriated suite; surveys his tackle; sets the globes spinning, one, two.

He descends the steps to the workshop floor. Workmen are assembling the new issue of the magazine. Pain gathers a copy, thumbs through it as he heads for the bookstore. Stops at the counter, suddenly focused on a piece towards the back. Reads, elated at first, then increasingly less happy. Aitken appears from the office.

AITKEN: Ah, ye found your piece. I thought that'd surprise ye ...

PAIN: *(A glance)* Aye.

AITKEN: Ye don't appear very happy ...

PAIN: This isn't what I wrote.

AITKEN: My friend Dr Rush made a number of suggestions for improvement, he's something of an expert in the field in question ...

PAIN: I see. *(Silence)* And was it your friend Dr Rush suggested my name might be improved by the addition of a final 'e'?

AITKEN: What? Let me look. *(Pain shows him the copy, moves off to open the store)* Ach, these blasted printers ...

PAIN: *(Returning)* No matter. I like it. New life, new name.

Aitken fumes off into the printroom. Tom Paine stoops again over the page, pen in hand; begins restoring what he wrote.

Close shots: the master printer's hand gathers characters into his stick; transfers to galley tray; to stone imposing-table; to iron-frame chase; to pressbed. Paine watches closely, eyes alive. The page is shimmed into make-ready. A journeyman beater spreads ink from a marble slab with a pair of leather-covered ink-balls onto the waiting type. The master printer nods. The puller's huge hands close around the bar; heave. A page emerges: Paine collects it, lays it on desk to study it.

MASTER PRINTER: Put it right, have we, Mr Paine?

PAINE: Looks fine now, Joseph.

*Close shot of the page: **African Slavery in America by Thomas Paine**.*

Paine's face, small smile.

***The Printer's Tavern**, mid-afternoon. Dense with diners and drinkers. A hot spring day. Town and back-country revellers reel past the open doorway and windows, en* *route for Spring Fair. Paine stands at the bar settling the table bill as he waits for nine ale mugs and a cordial glass to be refilled. He looks over at his table in the corner, where Aitken's printworkers are getting happy over their Spring Fair free pie and ale. They've pinned front pages of the new issue on walls and posts around them, a tiny altar to their work. Will is perched on a stool in their midst, stolidly crunching pie, eyes glued on Paine at the counter. Paine gives him a wink. A man approaches from a nearby table. He's mid-forties, slender, almost frail; black coat, grey britches and stockings; no frills, no buckles, no wig; long strawy hair tied at nape in a small mourning ribbon; gentle voice, thin flecks of German.*

MAN: Mr Paine? My name's Rittenhouse. A pleasure, sir.

PAINE: How do.

RITTENHOUSE: *(Calm, simple)* I very much admire the new direction you have given the paper.

PAINE: *(With respect)* Thank you.

RITTENHOUSE: *(A glance around the room, then quietly)* A group of friends gather Fridays at my house for open discussion. Ye'd be most welcome, sir.

PAINE: Rittenhouse, ye said? David Rittenhouse.? *(The man nods)* You built your own telescopes and followed the transit of Venus back in '69, am I right? I read your report. *(A smile)* I'd be honoured, sir.

RITTENHOUSE: *(A nod)* 7th and Mulberry.

He returns to his table. Paine lays out coins for his completed order; gazes again at the receding Rittenhouse.

Aitken's deserted printroom. *Afternoon; light fading. From the streets, the din of music, fun, growing release contends with the voices of street preachers calling down everlasting fire from their God of Wrath. Paine lets himself into the deserted printroom. Climbs steps to gallery. Peter, the young store assistant, appears in archway to front shop.*

PETER: Will I lock up, Mr Paine ...?

PAINE: I'll see to it, Peter, you get away, ye'll miss the fun ...

*The door bell rings as someone enters the bookshop;
Peter peels off to see to it.*

*Paine enters his new lodging, stock cleared, his own
meagre gear placed around room. Moves through to tiny
sleeping quarter beyond. Removes coat, loosens shirt,
finds pipe by bed, reaches into a bag beneath the wooden
cot for his pouch, comes up with Philly's stays. Stares at
them a moment. Finds pouch. Returns to outer room. Sits
at desk. Checks his day-book. Thunder bounces towards
the city; dies.*

Close shot of day-book: **Wednesday pm. Mr M
Oldenburg. 'On Women.' Discuss.** *Finds manuscript in
query file. Lights pipe as he checks it out.*

PETER: *(Below)* Mr Paine ... Your visitor's arrived.

Paine moves onto gallery. Peter's struggling into his coat.

PETER: In the office.

PAINE: *(A wink)* Enjoy Spring Fair.

PETER: Mr Aitken's back from New York. Went home.
Bad head.

*A dull bang of thunder, closer now. Paine nods. Peter
leaves. Paine collects the manuscript and coat, heads for
the front. Crosses the closed store to the counter-office.*

PAINE: *(In doorway)* Mr Oldenb ...

*A woman turns from the office window at his call; smiles.
She's around 30, pale, tall, strong-bodied, ashen-haired,
simply dressed.*

WOMAN: *(Some German there)* Mr Paine, is it? Marthe
Oldenburg, I used my maiden name, I hoped it would
sound more interesting ... Thank you for asking me to
come ...

PAINE: *(Off balance)* Forgive me, I'd expected a man. Please ...

He indicates a chair. She sits. He takes Aitken's chair at the desk, lays his jacket on a stool, recovering balance. Rebuttons his shirt. Stares at her.

PAINE: More interesting than what, Mrs ...?

MARTHE: Daley.

PAINE: Mm.

MARTHE: I married an Irishman. Swamp fever took him, last summer.

PAINE: Forgive me, I had not ...

MARTHE: Please. It happened, it can be spoken of.

Paine looks down at the manuscript on the desk. Notices her fingers turning the silver wedding band. Takes Aitken's money box from a drawer. Lays out nine silver half-joes on the desk top.

PAINE: I'll take it. That's four and sixpence, count it. *(She stares at him startled)* One, it's quite good. Two ...

MARTHE: ... Is it?

PAINE: The English needs some helping, but yes. Two, it's the first work we've had from a woman. Three, it'll be our first piece about women ...

Marthe collects the coins; holds them over her open purse.

MARTHE: I do not look for charity, Mr Paine.

PAINE: Nor shall you find it, Mrs Daley.

Slow smiles. Silence. A sense of drawnness hovers.

PAINE: Have you written other pieces?

MARTHE: No. I don't know why I wrote that. I've kept a day-book since I was twelve, the year I came here.

PAINE: I'd like to read it.

24

MARTHE: *(Eyes down)* No, no, it's a ... personal thing.

Thunder clouts the heavy air above the city. She looks away, at the window. Paine gazes at her.

PAINE: I have made a note or two ... *(She looks back at him - he's holding the manuscript)* Will we work on it?

MARTHE: Now, you mean?

PAINE: If you'd care to.

She wants it; it scares her to prudence.

MARTHE: I left my daughter with a neighbour, she's ... Thunder scares her.

PAINE: *(Standing; gentle)* Then you must go at once. Another time ...

MARTHE: *(Rising)* Thank you.

He smiles; leads her to the front door. She gazes at the packed bookshelves. A church bell begins to toll across the city. A second joins it.

PAINE: *(Unlocking door)* Let me know when you're free to set to, Mrs Daley. Bring your daughter with you, she can help at the counter ...

MARTHE: She's five, Mr Paine.

PAINE: She can stand on a box.

He holds the door for her. They look at each other in silence for some moments. The church bells grow gradually more urgent; more join them; the noise swells, edges towards menace.

PAINE: What is it?

MARTHE: They call the people. I think there must be a danger.

Folk call to each other in the streets. Paine looks out. When he looks back, she's gone. He scans the street for her. Thunder again. The bells dole out their sombre meanings. He grabs his coat from the office.

Dusk. Images of the moment around the city:

On the Common, *Spring Fair slowly gives way to listening silence, a maypole swings slowly to a stop. Men and women stare down on the summons, faces made grave by fear. A large man wrestling a pig kneels up to listen; the pig's teeth slice up at him, blood gouts from his ear.*

At Dock Creek, *young swimmers, lads and lasses, stand in the settling water, arrested in play. On the bush-lined banks, lovers and drunks lie in their separate oblivions.*

In a Recruiting Tent, *a huge militia captain, Timothy Matlack, in the makeshift uniform of the Philadelphia Associators, the semi-legal self-defence force paid for by the City, stops to listen with the rest. A stocky Scots recruiter, James Cannon, appears at the flap. The captain nods, moves out onto the Common.*

The State House Yard. *Paine hurries through the crowd converging on the State House. People walk fast, purposeful, concerned, without panic. Kids and dogs run on, smelling excitement. Fine carriages arrive from the outskirts, clogging the streets. Some way ahead, the State Yard's already jammed; walls, trees, roofs are being climbed for vantage. The bells begin to peal down to the one high above in the State House. On its wide balcony, Pennsylvania Assembly leaders and civic dignitaries are all but mustered.*

Paine heads for the Yard wall; gets a helping mitt from Matlack, the bear-like militia captain, already up there. The streets behind them are choked with people, standing, watching.

The bell stops. Voices die. Paine checks the balcony figures. Robert Morris arrives, brilliant in beaver coat, huddles to confer with others already out. A gaunt ancient carrying the HouseSpeaker's ceremonial staff appears, a second man in travel-stained dress in tow. More huddling. Unease begins to seep through the waiting crowd. Voices lift here and there for news.

PAINE: *(To Matlack)* What news, do you know?

The militia captain doesn't answer at once, busy contacting groups of men in the Yard below, little nods, finger signals, waves of a grubby kerchief. We recognise one of them: Cannon, the Scots recruiter.

MATLACK: *(Eventually; not looking; hoarse)* Uhunh. But those buggers're so scared up there, they're bumpin' into each other, so it ain't gonna be good. *(Fast; huge-voiced)* FOR GOD'S SAKE, **LET'S HEAR IT** . WE ARE GATHERED!

His contacts in the Yard take up the call, spread it beyond. The balcony people still appear unready to start, perhaps waiting for someone. Pressure grows from below.

The gaunt ancient HouseSpeaker steps forward abruptly, raises an arm for silence, bangs his staff twice on the floor.

HOUSESPEAKER: The Speaker of this House calls this meeting to order. May the good Lord guide us. *(Amens stutter across the great crowd, as translations below trail the balcony English.)* People of Pennsylvania, ye're summoned to hear a new-fetched letter from the Congress of Massachusetts on recent happenings in that beleaguered and most misfortunate colony. Our friend here have rode four days and nights fetching it. I ask you to listen with your customary calm and fortitude, secure in the knowledge that we ourselves face no present danger nor threat of one by these events ... *(Checks a slip of paper)* Mister ... *(Relieved to spot a tall, distinguished man hurrying out onto the balcony)* Ah, State President Dickenson.

The crowd tenses as the grandees go into more huddles. House servants carry lamps out, to light the crowded balcony. Paine scans the sombre Yard: spots his print workers; the Baches; Mrs Downey; Aitken; Rittenhouse, his wife and two young daughters; Will on a window ledge; and back to the captain.

27

PAINE: What now?

MATLACK: *(Harsh)* ... That's our State President, Half-Way Dickenson, he's worried this ain't bein' managed proper, he don't want them rebel Massachusetts people talking straight out to Pennsylvania folk, we might just get the Big Idea ... *(Paine frowns a question. The Captain grins, drops his voice to a hoarse whisper)* Independence! S'a word ye gotta whisper just now, 'less ye want yer neck stretchin', but it's comin', friend, it's comin' ...

HOUSESPEAKER: *(Backtracking)* ... Friends, let us first welcome President John Dickenson, who has an opinion to set before you on behalf of Council ... *(**Boos**, cries of' '**No, we will hear the news**' stop him in his tracks. Another brief flustered consultation. Robert Morris steps forward, lays a decisive word in Dickenson's ear. The balcony accepts its defeat)* Very well ... *(The swarthy Massachusetts man steps forward again, letter in hand. Thunder, a touch more distant. The deep, straining silence resumes.)* Mr Revere ...

REVERE: *(Reading; French Huguenot origins in the tough craftsman's voice)* From the Council, Congress and People of the colony of Massachusetts, to all Americans: We send hard news. Last Monday, April nineteenth, in the forenoon, at the town of Lexington, a body of some six hundred British Regulars, sent out under orders to disarm the people, being met on the common by a small band of townsfolk determined to defend their honour and their liberty, did, upon the command of their officers, deliberately take aim and fire upon that defenceless muster, leaving eight dead and many more wounded.

He looks up from the page. He's weeping. In the Yard below, people have begun to pray, others hug their dear ones closer. Faces register the new gravity of things. Paine's is stunned, uncomprehending.

REVERE: ... What happened next, how townships were pillaged, old men, women, children dragged onto the streets and publicly violated, houses burned and several hundred Americans attacked and mutilated, we must needs leave for a later occasion, in the hope that a few grains of truth may fill a whole barn with justice ...

He pauses again, to wipe his glasses and shield the paper from the sifting rain just begun. In close up, Paine burns with the news, eyes chilled with the dawning horror. Matlack chews on, impassive. Most folk stand whitely in the rain, aghast, borne down. A blind old man, heavy Swedish accent, calls **Is he done?** *Someone quietens him. Town lamplighters move around the edges of the vast throng, lighting up. Torches flare here and there inside the crowd.*

REVERE: *(Reading on)* ... Fellow Americans, we ask these questions: If this be not Tyranny, how shall we name it? And if this be not War, how shall it be called? Fellow Americans, the crisis is come, the time to rise is upon us, and the fate not of a colony but of a **continent** hangs on your answer. Signed, John Hancock, President, Sam Adams, John Adams, Executive Members.

Revere sniffs, blows his nose. Translation tails away. The balcony stands mute, frozen in indecision, aware of the power of feeling below. Fragments of prayer lift, fall: fear, grief, foreboding rise like steam from the silence. A contact hands a flaming torch to Matlack, still by Paine on the wall.

REVERE: ... Made up a rough list o' dead 'n' wounded ...

VOICE: ... I got a boy there, town o' Quincy. William Malley ...

Other names are called; more. Revere turns to the balcony grandees for guidance.

REVERE: Simpler if I just read them out ...

The HouseSpeaker stands forward, bangs his stick. The names die away.

HOUSESPEAKER: Calm yourselves, fellow citizens. I call now President ...

MATLACK: *(Big)* Let their names be heard ...

HOUSESPEAKER: ... John Dickenson to the floor.

MATLACK: *(Full fury)* Shame on your head. We are **all** family here, not a man murdered but we lose a brother.

The HouseSpeaker clouts the balcony repeatedly with his stick. Dickenson waits with demonstrated patience.

MATLACK: What are ye up there? Americans? Or sacks of British snot dumped on us while we sleep to keep us in our place?

HOUSESPEAKER: *(Over the din)* President John Dickenson has the floor.

DICKENSON: *(As things subside)* Friends, the agitator there who seeks to disturb our solemn meeting ... is, of course, Mr Hothead Matlack. *(Gentry in the Yard fill the space he leaves them with hissing and calls of derision)* The name speaks for itself ...

MATLACK: All ends against the middle, is it, Mr Half-Way bloody Dickenson? The game's up, man. Ye'll see soon enough.

He gives a shrill whistle, lips on teeth, drops down into the street, torch in hand, headed off. Groups of working men begin to push out from the Yard to follow, some of Paine's printworkers among them. Paine watches, tense, unsure: sees Rittenhouse leave his family abruptly, push after them.

DICKENSON: *(Soothing tones)* My friends, as ye know, we seek peace and justice through negotiated settlement with our British cousins ... And no bully may deflect us from our chosen path ...

Paine's eyes follow the exodus of Matlack's people to a corner warehouse, where they angrily regroup. Rittenhouse reaches them; begins to argue with Matlack, restrain him. The Scots recruiter arrives, tries to mediate.

Paine scans the warehouse block. Sees Marthe Daley, on a tea chest, face greasy with tears, watching the balcony. He watches her until she sees him. A moment between them, a graveness shared. She gets down, disappears into the crowd. Paine looks back at the corner warehouse: the radicals are gone. Dickenson soothes on. Paine turns back to him.

DICKENSON: ... Fellow Pennsylvanians, like many here I'm but a simple farmer, but I do know that He who made us will always heed the call of a troubled soul. *(Pause)* I ask the Reverend William Smith, Provost of our great college here, to lead us in a final prayer.

Silence, as translations tail away; the fat, creamy cleric waddles forward, bible in hand, under a parasol borne by a black liveried slave. Approving nods from other grandees, on the brink of another Balcony victory.

SMITH: Let us pray. O Lord ...

The old man's voice sets up in Swedish from below, addressing the balcony. The Speaker stands forward, bangs his staff, Dickenson restrains him: no danger there. The old man talks stolidly on.

DICKENSON: In English, if you please, sir.

YOUNG WOMAN: *(Swedish in her English)* My papa say he came in from Lancaster for Spring Fair, he wanna know why we not hear more 'bout these murderings ...

DICKENSON: Well, I do believe we have dealt with them, tell him ...

The old Swede speaks on.

YOUNG WOMAN: ... He's saying did our people give back fire or just stood for shooting ...?

The crowd lifts a little, behind the question. Revere stands forward again.

REVERE: Yeah, we returned fire all right ...

He's checking his notebook.

YOUNG WOMAN: My father's asking how many we get?

REVERE: Well, er, we think 'bout two hundred and seventy Redcoats killed 'n' a lot more hit.

Silence. The crowd stirs, half lifted further, half more depressed. The old guy rattles on.

YOUNG WOMAN: My father thanks you, mister. Says he don't like no-one shot an' he aint no scholar ... but he reckon if the British have a couple more victories like this one, we'll have them on their knees beggin' for peace ...

Silence for a while, as folk do their sums. Then a slow swell of chuckling laughter sets up; applause. Faces gleam from the bright dark; grow slowly grave again.

Paine's face, watching, listening, finding himself at last at one with these people and their purpose. Smith resumes the prayer. Paine again, his hand straying unbidden to the wooden pen he carries as craft-sign on his lapel. He looks down at the hand, the pen. Climbs from the wall. The prayer lards on. He leaves.

Fade sound. Bring up the sound of a side-drum, a slow solemn roll; over it, Paine's writing voice:

PAINE'S VOICE: ... Whoever considers the unprincipled enemy we have to cope with will not hesitate to declare that nothing but arms or miracles can reduce them to reason or moderation, for they have lost sight of the limits of humanity ...

City streets, *early May evening.*

Thousands stand in respectful silence as the thirteen delegations to the Continental Congress process into town. A single muffled bell marks the gravity; a single kettledrum marks their passage. James Cannon, in full militia uniform, calls out the names of each contingent from a wall at the city gates, as the camera frames the key people: Patrick Henry, Richard Henry Lee, Arthur Lee, Thomas Jefferson, from Virginia; Gouverneur Morris,

John Jay, from New York; John Witherspoon, New Jersey; John Hancock, Sam and John Adams, Massachussetts; Henry Laurens, North Carolina.

PAINE'S VOICE: ... Could the peaceable principles of the Quakers be universally established, arms and the art of war would be wholly extirpated. But we live not in a world of angels ...

Paine's living space in Aitken's shop, *evening. Paine at his window desk, in a fury of writing. Through his first-floor window we see the delegations process on down crowded Walnut Street towards the State House.*

PAINE'S VOICE: ... I am thus far a Quaker that I would gladly agree with all the world to lay aside the use of arms and settle matters by negotiation ...

He looks up as a last group appears, on horseback: four militia officers, led by Colonel Washington, in the green and blue uniform of Virginia, on a short black horse. He looks straight ahead, face impassive, jaw clenched. People in the crowd note him, not sure who he is but sensing importance.

PAINE'S VOICE: ... but unless the whole will, the matter ends, and I take up my musket and thank heaven he has put it in my power.

Paine finishes, dries the ink, gathers his pages. His eyes return to the scene in the streets: Washington and escort are held up by a bunch of cows strayed from market, his horse gets skittery, he stills it, no fuss. Paine takes the stairs to printshop, checks for signs of Aitken, lays the pages on the office desk for his return. Joseph appears in doorway.

JOSEPH: All done, is it? *(Paine nods)* Will I take it?

PAINE: Aitken's asked to see it. Jumpy. *(Another Congress carriage passes, to applause)* All this trouble around. Sarah well?

JOSEPH: Coping.

PAINE: When's she due?

JOSEPH: Coupla months, but she's in no hurry, not with a war brewin'.

PAINE: Ye think so?

JOSEPH: Don't you? *(Turns to leave)* David Rittenhouse dropped by, left ye a note, s'on the counter there ...

PAINE: Thanks, Joe.

JOSEPH: We start putting up Monday.

He's gone. Paine moves out to the counter, gathers his coat, finds the letter; opens it. A boat siren sounds, a distance away. He squints at the note; sniffs; leaves.

The docks. *Evening. Ben Franklin, the people's own returned, debarking from the London packet to cheers and applause from the packed wharves. He walks the line of welcoming civic dignitaries, a legendary 70 year old shambles with a limp, kidney stones and seriously dishevelled dress, smiling on all as he works the line.*

Paine watches from the quayside as the great man's shown to his State House carriage. Franklin sees him, breaks away from his handlers to shake his hand. Onlookers crane to see who it might be.

FRANKLIN: Thomas Paine, as I live and breathe.

PAINE: Welcome home, Mr Franklin ...

FRANKLIN: I'm never sent for but there's a crisis. Summoned to knock a few heads together before our blessed Congress starts tearing itself to pieces. How are ye? Heard ye were sick.

PAINE: I'm well, Mr Franklin. Begun to feel at home.

FRANKLIN: *(Eyeing him)* Thought ye might. My son-in-law there ... *(Nods head to his rear; Paine sees Bache, self-importantly a member of the Reception Committee)* ... Mr Bache ... wrote me ye were scribblin' contentious pieces for the public presses.

PAINE: ... Tryin' to, aye ...

FRANKLIN: ... In his judgment quite odious ...

PAINE: ... Guess it's a free country. *(A moment)* Or will be.

Silence. They eye each other.

FRANKLIN: Gimme a day or two, I'd like a word, drop by
the house, came by something in France might interest
ye ... *(He winks, turns, waves to the crowd, scrambles
up into the carriage. To the African coachman)* Take
me home, sir. Don't spare the holly ...

*Paine watches the coach clatter off. Turns to look at the
dignitaries, sees Dickenson, the HouseSpeaker, Bache, all
miffed the great man's gone without their speeches of
welcome, pissed at Paine.*

Same day. Dusk. The interior of a tavern. *Through the
window we see Rittenhouse's corner cottage on Mulberry.
Shadowy figures arrive, ones and twos; then a carriage: a
cloaked figure steps out, goes inside.*

*Paine watches as he finishes his pie and ale. Looks down
at Rittenhouse's note on the table by his hand: we read*
Now's the time. Nine tonight. DR. *A town clock begins to
strike. He drains his beaker. Lays coins on the table.
Pockets the note.*

Mulberry Street. *Paine begins to cross the street, is held
up by a Dad's Army straggle of militia trying to march in
step down the middle of the road. A gaggle of kids follow
them, much amused. Finally across, he passes the waiting
carriage; glimpses a man inside, working on a sheaf of
documents by candlelight; approaches the front door to
knock, the door swings abruptly open, Aitken's Master-
printer steps out, struggling into his coat.*

PAINE: Joseph ...?

JOSEPH: *(Sotto)* Mr Paine, good to have ye here, they're
just begun, ye'll have to excuse me, gotta hurry Mr
Adams there to another meeting, driver don't know the
way ...

He leaves. The carriage takes off at pace; Paine frowns, surprised. Knocks at door. Hannah Rittenhouse answers.

PAINE: Thomas Paine, ma'am.

HANNAH: Does my husband expect ye?

PAINE: *(Hands her the note)* I believe so.

He follows her in, she disappears into a room, he waits in the tiny hallway. Voices: meeting underway. A beautiful clock ticks relentlessly by the stair: he studies it. It's a Rittenhouse.

HANNAH: *(Back out)* Aye, ye're welcome, Thomas Paine, but I warn ye, we have a grand speaker from up north in tonight, so it's a crush.

She holds the door for him. The room's packed. Ten or fifteen men sit round a table, as many more crowd the walls. Rittenhouse, at table, gives Paine a welcoming nod. A man he can't quite see is already launched, the smoky room giving him tense attention. Paine angles, back to wall, to get a view; spots Matlack; then the speaker; Sam Adams.

SAM ADAMS: *(50s; greying; nights without sleep; tireless)* ... So here it is. The gospel according to Sam Adams. "Should go to war, shouldn't go to war" ain't the issue any more. Boston's an occupied city under martial law, our Parliament summarily suspended, our courts shut down, our commonwealth ruled by the diktat of an English Lord, and thirty thousand soldiers and eighty cannon to make his point, put there by a London Parliament to protect the goldmine we have become for them ... The British are waging war on America **already**, after us it'll be New York, after New York Philadelphia, a mouthful at a time, colony after colony, just how they like us ... *(He gazes at the lamplit faces around the room. Paine's burns in the shadows, listening intently)* Seems to me we have but two choices, friends. We can surrender to this tyranny, wait in line for our turn to come ... Or we can resist it. We

36

can fall back under their yoke. Or defend ourselves. Roll over or fight. *(Another glance at his audience, gauging the levels of support and unease.)* But if we choose resistance, we must **all** choose it, thirteen clocks striking at once, one **continental** entity, one army, one command, one purpose. All. Together. *(Checks notes a moment. Men's coughs, sniffs, looks, fill the tense silence.)* Now here's the rub. Virginia and Massachusetts have tabled a motion calling for all Colonial militias to be engrossed into a new Continental Army. Nine of the thirteen delegations are behind us, the rest are HalfWayhousing, waiting on Pennsylvania to get off the fence, your esteemed leaders are wavering, one more push from below, friends, and we can all go forward together ...

MATLACK: Leave it to us, Mr Adams, we'll get the people out, they're ready all right.

SAM ADAMS: Does my soul good to hear it, Mr Matlack. And in return, I make ye a solemn promise: you boys deliver Pennsylvania for unity, we'll have the grandest and fairest revolution there ever was ... *(The room comes vividly to life; growls of appreciation, fists pump the table)* Who's that, that Jim Cannon down there?

CANNON: *(The recruiter; thick Scots)* Aye, that it is, Mr Adams.

ADAMS: Long way from Edinburgh, Jim. Bedded in, are ye?

CANNON: I am, sir. Like grit in an oyster.

Adams chuckles; some laughter spreads. His eyes wander the room; meet Paine's eventually; move on. We stay with Paine.

Cut to the interior of Rittenhouse's workshop at the back of the house. Night. Paine's face, lamp-lit, watching. We see brass planets, earth, moon, sun float in silent perfect order before his rapt gaze.

Paine's point of view of the planetarium. Rittenhouse's face moves into shot; just arrived in the room from seeing folk out. They look at each other across the orrery for several moments.

PAINE: You do this? *(Gets a nod)* Perfect.

RITTENHOUSE: Will be. One day. *(Moves a second lamp in)* What kept ye? Asked ye here months back ...

PAINE: Guess I was finding my way.

RITTENHOUSE: So. Ready to take a part, are ye?

PAINE: 'Pends what ye got in mind. Ain't much of a speaker ...

RITTENHOUSE: Sam Adams reckons the next step's for someone to sit down and tell Americans what's at stake here. *(He makes a writing motion with his hand)*. I told him he should look no further. *(Paine blinks)* He agreed.

PAINE: Sam Adams ...? Sam Adams wouldn't know me from a hole in the road, how would he know ...?

RITTENHOUSE: Ain't a piece printed here Sam Adams don't read. He'd know all right. *(A young girl calls from sleep in the next room. He turns to listen. She's quiet.)* Ye spoken with Mr Franklin yet?

PAINE: *(Slowly; working things out)* ... Franklin? Ye mean ... Mr Franklin's part o' this ... *(the group, the meeting, the movement)* ... party to it ...?

RITTENHOUSE: *(Softly)* Ask him.

The young girl cries again. Rittenhouse takes a lamp to comfort her. Paine watches a moment through the open doorway. Rittenhouse shushes her in his gentle arms.

Paine looks back at the world again. The spring is all but unwound, the brass universe hovering to a stop.

Philadelphia city streets. *Day. People are out in their hundreds, taking the air and testing the political temperature. Paine strides purposefully through the moil, headed for Franklin's place on Market Street. His path's* *half-blocked by an impromptu sidewalk meeting, a sizeable crowd spilling out onto the roadway. He catches sight of Matlack, up on a box, pushing the Sam Adams Unity line; spots several of the men at the Rittenhouse meeting passing out handbills. He takes one, reads it as he heads on. We see: Unity is Strength - Pennsylvania Must Decide ...*

Franklin's house. *Ben Franklin stands at a front window, watching the Unity Meeting at the corner of the street. In the room behind him, sounds of men's voices at work on something. He spots Paine emerge on the other side of the street, wait for a carriage to pass before crossing to the house. Franklin turns back into the room with a smile, shuffles towards the door. Robert Morris and a second man, on the sharp side of dandy, sit at a table filled with documents on the far side of the room, making extensive calculations using abacus, pencil and paper. They look up as the door sounds.*

FRANKLIN: Ye'll excuse me, gentlemen ... Help yourselves to the port.

He heads down the hall to answer. Sees Paine at the bottom of the steps.

FRANKLIN: Am I expectin' ye ...?

PAINE: Bad time, is it?

FRANKLIN: *(Grins)* 'Pends what ye got to say for yourself. Come in.

Paine follows him in. A househelp plods up the passage to answer the door.

FRANKLIN: It's done, go back to the sherry ...

HOUSEHELP: *(Passing them)* You run the country. I answer doors. That's the deal.

He bangs the door closed. Franklin chuckles. Mutters "Ah America, don't ye love it", ambles back into the meeting room. Paine stops in the doorway. The two stare across at him.

FRANKLIN: This here's Thomas Paine - Robert Morris, Silas Deane - *(Nods exchanged)*. Make a note of the name, gentlemen, be sure it won't be the last ye'll hear of it. I'll be over the way there for a wee while, should ye require arbitration ...

He smiles, a radiance, leads Paine across the hall to his study, books on all walls, practical experiments on every surface: Merlin's den.

FRANKLIN: Close the door, rest yer legs, there's something I've been meaning to do ... *(He takes a book from a shelf, begins inscribing the title page. Sees Paine hovering by the offered chair. As he writes)* Sit ye down, man, no need to worry about the two fine fellers in the other room, they're like dogs in a boneyard just now, Congress is considering sending a delegation to France looking for loans and ... *(Squints a look at Paine across the desk)* such materials as the Crisis might put us in need of, Mr Morris would be the Money, Mr Deane the Agent-in-Chief, they're selflessly donating an afternoon to the calculation of their potential profits. Ah Business! *(Dusts the ink dry, closes the book.)* Here. *(Hands it him.)* Looked to give ye this in London, remember? *(Paine nods, checks the spine; smiles his thanks).* So. What can I do for ye, friend?

Paine takes out a bulky envelope, lays it on the desk.

FRANKLIN: What is it?

PAINE: It's thirty pounds. The loan ye made me for the passage out ...

FRANKLIN: No interest?

PAINE: Erm. No ...

Franklin picks it up, as if weighing it, puts it down.

FRANKLIN: What else?

PAINE: Ye read any o' my pieces, Mr Franklin?

FRANKLIN: Couple, aye.

PAINE: Any good?

FRANKLIN: Well, they won't be troubling Shakespeare, but they'll do. Why d'ye ask?

PAINE: There's people pressing me to write something, pamphlet, book ... substantial anyway. Give up what I'm doin' and work for the ... cause, I guess.

FRANKLIN: The cause bein' our liberties ...? *(Paine nods)* So what's the rub? It don't appeal ...?

PAINE: Appeals fine. Guess I'm vain as the next man. I'm not sure I'm up to the task.

FRANKLIN: 'Cos ye're not Shakespeare ...?

PAINE: I can handle that. 'Cos I can't write to order. What I write's gotta come out o' me, not a committee. Can't be writing to instruction ...

FRANKLIN: Whoa there. S'that what ye think these folks're lookin' for, a tame critter with a pen for hire ...?

PAINE: No, I ain't sayin'...

FRANKLIN: ... An' if they were, why in the Maker's name would they come to you, orneriest cuss I ever met ...? I don't know who these folk are, don't want to, but if ye'd like my twopennorth, they came to **you** because ye write well, in a language common folk understand, and because you're the only man of talent hereabouts who's ready to put the truth before his own neck. In a word, they trust ye. As do I. To wit ... *(He reaches into a drawer, hands him a fat document folder stuffed with papers. It carries an embossed British Crown; has SECRET TO THIS MINISTRY stamped across it.)* Ask no questions about this, I've never seen it in my life, the secret papers inside detail some fairly gruesome contingency schemes for dealing with these colonies, should we look to disburden ourselves of British Rule. Tek 'em, use 'em or no, s'all one. Ye'll do what ye do and it'll do. *(Checks his watch; rises.)* Anything else? I'd best get back 'fore those buggers empty the till ...

Paine stuffs the book into his satchel. Stares hard at the secret file. Touches it. Picks it up. Places it with the book. Franklin gathers the envelope Paine placed on his desk. Holds it out.

PAINE: What's that?

FRANKLIN: Might come in handy for expenses, if ye find yourself strugglin' with an oeuvre. Ye can bring it back another time. With interest. Find yer own way, will ye?

He means to the door. Other meanings hover. Paine takes it; sniffs; leaves.

Aitken's printworks. *Morning. Click and hum of printworkers setting up the new issue. Joseph supervises as he prepares ink for the run; flicks occasional looks at Paine by a table, just up, hair a mess, checking manuscripts, the frown on his face deepening as he reads.*

PAINE: *(Eventually)* 'S goin' on, Joe ...?

JOSEPH: *(A shrug)* Best ask the boss, Tom ...

Paine sniffs, carries an MS with him out towards the front office.

In the office, Aitken stands at the window, looking out on a turbulent streetmeeting. Matlack's familiar speaker's voice drums out the theme of Unity.

PAINE: *(Arriving)* Ye pulled my article ...?

AITKEN: *(Returning to desk)* I did, Mr Paine. There's a price to pay for publishing treason, your neck's yer own affair, but I'm quite attached to mine ...

PAINE: And the **public** interest counts for nothing ...?

AITKEN: Good God, man, use yer common sense. *(Holds up the offending MS)* "Thoughts on a Defensive War"!? Offering moral and political argument in favour of war against the King??!! It's not only treasonous, it's lunatic. Ye think for one minute the folk out there share yer crackwit vision of the future? "New World, America ..."? When common sense tells 'em there's no future at all in a handful of farmers takin' on the military might of the most powerful nation on the planet ... Look, I don't want to fall out, Tom, yer work's valued, I mean that, but this here's my life. Print this, they take my licence, my liberty, mebbe my ... *(Feels his collar)* If it's the public interest or my neck, I reckon I know where I stand. We go with the new piece...

PAINE: *(Thinks; looks down at the fillpiece in his hand)* I could forgive ye much, Mr Aitken, being wrong's not a crime, not even being wrong about **every**thing, though it comes close, but ... *(Reads.)* ... "Philadelphia, Fairest of Cities, by A Gentleman of Scotland ..."??!! You, right? *(Reads on)* "Prepare to salute, O gentle reader, in the fairest of colonies this noblest of cities, where yes, it must be agreed, all our geese are indeed swans"... Ye had the gall to drop my piece for **this** horseshit ...? *(He throws the paper on the desk)* I've seen better writing on painted pisspots. And if them's yer standards from now on, ye'll be bankrupt 'fore ye've time to fill one ...

He leaves. Aitken sits there, wheyfaced, upset. Crosses to the window, stares grimly out, chews at his lip. Sounds from street; disturbance, shouts, running.

City streets, *morning, some days later. Paine searches for new lodgings, Will helping with bags and globes.*

PAINE'S WRITING VOICE: The laying of a country desolate with fire and sword, and declaring war against the natural rights of all mankind, is the concern of every man to whom nature hath given the power of feeling.

By the State House, they stop to watch Washington's High Command hove into view: Lee, Schuyler, Reed and Mifflin flank their General, brilliant on his fine new white horse.

WILL: What's he call' ?

PAINE: That's General Washington. Wouldn't think so by the face on 'im, but he just got himself an army ...

Midtown, several Landladies turn him down, frowning at his appearance and the presence of Will.

They've arrived at a small house on Walnut. A pale-haired girl of five or so answers the knock.

PAINE: Is your father here? *(She frowns, shakes her head)* What about your mama?

She disappears into the house. Will's studying a globe.

PAINE: Africa.

Will turns till he finds it. Paine nods.

PAINE'S WRITING VOICE: ... The cause of America is in great measure the cause of all mankind ...

The girl returns, speaking as she comes.

GIRL: Mama says if it's the room it's two dollars and a half a week, washing and eating's extra, she's making bread ... S'that?

Paine crouches, shows her the globe.

PAINE: S'the world.

GIRL: *(Touching it)* Why's it round like that?

PAINE: *(A grin)* Same reason a wheel's round, or your spinnin' top, world's made for turnin'...

A woman's dress has filled the space beyond the girl's head. He looks up from the crouch; sees Marthe Daley, sleeves rolled, dough in hands, staring down at him.

MARTHE: Forgive me, I thought it was the room ...

PAINE: *(Standing)* It is. I saw the notice. I did not know ...

MARTHE: *(Uncertain now)* I think it will be too small for your needs ...

PAINE: Will I look?

MARTHE: To the right.

She leads him in to the stairs, heads on to the kitchen, daughter in tow. Paine takes the stair. Enters the bright, modest room. Pushes through to a sort of box room beyond, empty save for a little metal-frame bed. Marthe appears in the outer room.

MARTHE: It **is** too small, yes?

PAINE: No. It's perfect.

MARTHE: What's the boy?

PAINE: He's a friend. He stays in town.

MARTHE: How long will you want it?

PAINE: Can't say. *(They're quite close, in the still room.)* I'd hoped you would call again.

MARTHE: No. I've been occupied. Making this ready for rent. *(Turning)* Lotte and me sleep there ... There's a sitting room below. Supper's at seven.

She leaves without looking. Paine looks at the room. Lifts a small table to the window. Places a lamp on it. Follows her down. Goes out to Will at the front door.

WILL: Good?

PAINE: Good.

WILL: Good.

Will holds out the globe.

PAINE: Remember where I am?

WILL: Ya.

PAINE: Take it. Come back next week, we'll see what you know.

Will looks at him warily. Nods. Heads off, clutching his globe. Paine turns. Stares at the house.

Marthe's house, *downstairs. Evening. Supper: Paine and Lotte sit at a table before bowls of stew. Marthe joins them with hers.*

MARTHE: Will you say grace, Mr Paine?

Their heads duck down over steepled hands. Paine's in trouble.

PAINE: We are glad to have this good food for our bellies, when so many on this earth stay empty ...

45

LOTTE: Amen.

MARTHE: *(Staring at him)* Amen.

Paine and Lotte eat. Marthe watches.

PAINE: Mmm.

LOTTE: Mmm.

Paine's room *in Marthe's house. Night. Window desk, lit lamp, paper, pen, ink, glass, rum.*

A page, a column of titles - Plain Talk Plain Truth True Talk Plain Sense - all struck out. Paine sits in a chair backed to the furthermost wall, staring at the desk and the task, a touch of fear in the eyes, weighing the enormity. A Town Clock strikes: two. He gets up abruptly, takes Secret File and Franklin's book from his satchel, lays them on desk. Flicks slowly through the file a moment, closes it. Sits. Pours a measure of rum. On impulse opens the book Franklin gave him: EPITAPH ON HIMSELF. Remembers the inscription, looks for it.

Reads, a mumble: "If you would not be forgotten, as soon as you are dead and rotten, either write things worth reading, or do things worth the writing. Godspeed in America. BF"

Paine dips his pen; ready. Scrawls a final title: COMMON SENSE on INDEPENDENCE.

Marthe's house. *A sequence of images, night and day. Weeks turn into months, as Paine struggles with the piece. Fragments of sentences voiced, breaking down to silence. Rum. Ink being mixed, paper smoothed. His face beards over, his hair grows lank. The room fills with manuscript; floor, bed, chests, cupboards, chairs.*

Layered in with the work, images of Paine and Marthe, in a slow unspoken coil of attraction and defensiveness. Paine working, watching Marthe as she hangs out washing on a tiny common plot behind the house: the pen stills; her strong arms reach for the line; sun on her neck; a breeze pushing her dress across her flanks.

*He watches Marthe from his doorway as she reads Lotte
to sleep. Wisps of Pilgrim's Progress reach him: he knows
it by heart. Marthe tiptoes from the room. Meets his eyes
on her on the landing. A moment. She retreats down the
stairs. He wants to follow; doesn't.*

Marthe's sitting room. *Night. She darns. Hears him on
the stair, picks up her bible, opens it before he appears.
He stoops with a taper before the fire to light his pipe.
Sits for a moment. Stares at her. She reads on, aware of
his eyes. A church clock strikes ten. She closes the book,
rubs her eyes, gathers her things.*

MARTHE: Will you take something, Mr Paine?

*He shakes his head. She takes a lamp, leaves for the
scullery. He waits a moment. Follows her. She's drinking
a scoop of water from the barrel. Sees him, dark in the
doorway.*

PAINE: *(Low)* A question.

MARTHE: What question?

PAINE: I'm almost done up there ... Would you sooner I
leave your house then?

MARTHE: *(Still, pale in the light)* Why? You feel
unwelcome here?

PAINE: I feel I set some unease in you, some discomfiture.
From the first day in the store and ever since,
something there is in me gives you ...

MARTHE: ... It is not in you, Mr Paine. *(Long silence)* It is
in me.

*She picks up the lamp. He steps to let her by. Closes his
eyes, takes in the waft of her strong body as she leaves.*

Paine's room, *night. His face as before, eyes closed, her
body in his nostrils. He resumes work. Desk. Rum. A fury
of writing, riding high energy displaced from sexual need.*

Lotte's voice, close by, calling him to wake.

*Late afternoon. Paine wakes on his bed, a wreck. Lotte
stands over him, in her mother's bonnet, shoes, and stays
over her dress.*

LOTTE: Gentleman come to see you. *(He struggles back to
the land of the living)* We gonna read later?

PAINE: I s'pose ... *(She's leaving)* Who are you today then?

LOTTE: *(Over shoulder)* The Queen of England.

PAINE: Make the most of it.

*Downstairs, Marthe talks in German with a couple of
neighbours at the front step. The two women stop to gawp as
Paine pads past them, bottle in hand, flowing hair and full
beard, like Blake's God the Father. He says Goodday, leaves
Marthe explaining the eccentric English lodger, enters the
sitting room. Rittenhouse turns from the window to greet him.
Blinks at Paine's appearance. Holds Paine's note up.*

RITTENHOUSE: It was good to hear you were ... still with
us. Is it done?

PAINE: About. You found me a printer?

*He flexes a painful writing hand. Rittenhouse re-studies
the note.*

RITTENHOUSE: Philadelphia appears right out of patriot
printers just now ... But Tim Matlack thinks he may
have a man. Wants you to meet him. Right away.

Paine frowns, not sure.

PAINE: What, right now ...?

RITTENHOUSE: Ja. I believe so.

*The front door closes, Marthe appears in their doorway.
Asks Rittenhouse in German if she can get him anything,
he answers in German, declining. She looks at Paine for a
moment, heads off for the scullery. Rittenhouse hands him
the day's "Philadelphia Packet."*

RITTENHOUSE: The King has proclaimed on us. We're a
rebellion: it's official.

Paine studies the page. Absorbs the enormity

PAINE: Where'll he be? Matlack?

RITTENHOUSE: Dog Inn. Race Street.

PAINE: I'll get myself ready ...

RITTENHOUSE: You know Race Street? *(Paine shakes head)* Take a stick. *(A small smile)* Otherwise ... *(Examines his appearance)* ... you'll do fine.

Paine smiles, pads off up stairs. Rittenhouse follows to the hall.

RITTENHOUSE: Tom. *(Paine turns)* Will I read it?

PAINE: Have to be here, ain't got but the one copy ...

RITTENHOUSE: *(Simple)* I have time.

PAINE: *(Warmed)* I'll fetch it.

Race Street. *Cold, black, early winter evening. Matlack leads Paine down Race Street, the unacceptable face of Philadelphia. Whores, pimps, rogues, sailors, deckmen, drunks, disgraced lawyers and derelicts possess the shitten streets: more London than America. Matlack's at home here, known, respected: talks as he moves through the moil.*

MATLACK: ... Name's Bell, not long here, has a shop in Southwark, won't risk you bein' seen there. Claims 'e's a patriot. I reckon 'e just needs the business. But believe it, we ain't 'xactly spoilt fer choice ...

He's turned down a short alley. Ahead, on waste ground, a bonfire, men gathered there in a rough arena. Matlack scans faces, approaches a short muffled figure in the circle. Paine peers over men's shoulders: two cocks are being matched in the flamelight. Matlack signals Paine to join him. Bell takes him in briefly, returns his gaze to the cocks.

PAINE: My friend tells me you might ...

BELL: *(Not looking; Welsh, from Pontypridd)* ... I might. Gorrit with ye?

PAINE: Uhunh.

BELL: Long, is it?

PAINE: Long enough.

BELL: Sorta run ye lookin' fer?

PAINE: Start wi' ten.

BELL: Thousand? *(Paine nods)* Jesus. *(Works stuff out)* I'll need to show it to a lawyer.

PAINE: Uhunh. You show it no-one.

Bell licks his lips. Looks briefly at Paine's firelit face. Rubs his fingers on his adam's apple.

BELL: Ye think the British've run outa rope, is it? *(He looks back at the cocks)* But I'm a patriot, every inch. I take costs and fifty percent, that's my deal.

Paine bites on his anger.

PAINE: Draw up your contract. Ye can send it through my friend there. But heed this: ye show it no one; ye change not a word.

A cock screams, blood spurts on the cobbles. Men move in for their winnings. Paine looks for Matlack; sees him collecting dollars from the promoter. Looks back at Bell: he's gone.

Paine's room *in Marthe's house. Evening. Marthe sits at his desk, making a fair copy of Paine's MS, mouthing and mulling passages with approval. Hears Lotte call from the back step, catches a glimpse out back of the returning Paine. Dries and gathers her work at speed, re-orders his, checks the desk is as it was, goes out onto the landing. Paine's coming through from the kitchen, Lotte in his arms.*

PAINE: Did he read it, Rittenhouse ...?

MARTHE: He did.

Paine puts Lotte down, tells her to fetch her book;

disappointed. Heads back to scullery. Marthe lays the copy pages in her bedroom, joins him in the back. He drinks a scoop of water.

PAINE: Did he say anything?

MARTHE: He did. *(He eyes her)* He said ye should lay low till it be published, and on no account put your own name to it.

PAINE: That all?

Lotte in, annoyed.

LOTTE: Can't find the goddamn thing, Mr Paine ...

Marthe throws some serious German at her for the swear-word. Lotte frowns, sulky, glancing at Paine.

PAINE: Wait, maybe I have it.

He heads for his room. Marthe and Lotte talk tersely on in German. He finds the Pilgrim's Progress on a shelf. Stops at the desk. Sees his name on the envelope laid on his manuscript. Opens it. His face, as he reads.

RITTENHOUSE'S VOICE: Tom, for what it's worth, the last time I felt like this I had just finished reading Newton's *Optics*. It will do, friend. And if it don't, we will not deserve a future. D.R.

Paine lays it down, relieved, happy. Marthe's voice lifts for a moment from the back of the house. Paine smells her here in the room. Stares at the desk for clues. Puts his finger on a spot of something, checks: wet ink. Frowns his puzzlement.

Walnut Street. *Bleak winter afternoon. Paine and Will sit under a canvas awning on the back-plot; Will's assembling a wooden model of some kind. Paine supervises as he shaves, almost finished: hair and beard lie in a mound at his feet. Marthe calls from the back door. Paine signals Will to cover the model, leaves for the house.*

MARTHE: *(Dressed for out)* We go now ...

Paine stops in the doorway. Sees Marthe buttoning Lotte's coat, two small packed bags on the table.

PAINE: Go where?

MARTHE: There's vittles in the pantry and Mrs Alberts will look to your loaves ... *(A glance)* We go to my husband's people at year's end, Mr Paine, I told you a week back, had you forgotten ...?

PAINE: *(Eyeing the bags)* I thought it was just the girl ...

MARTHE: I'll take supper there ... If it grows late, and dirty weather, I'll stay over. *(Pats her daughter)* There. Get your bag, say goodbye.

Lotte lugs her bag to Paine, who stoops to hug her; carries it on to the front door. Paine moves to the back door, depressed. Marthe squeezes her hands into little-used best gloves. Will appears at the back door, hands Paine the cloth-covered model and pipe.

WILL: I'll be wanted now.

PAINE: Aye.

WILL: Did the English gentleman find ye? Come askin' Ma Downey's yes'day.

PAINE: English gentleman? *(Eyes narrowing)* Ye din't tell 'im anythin'...? *(Will shakes his head. Paine nods.)* Thanks.

Will goes. Paine ponders the "English gentleman", a touch concerned. Marthe's ready. Eyes the covered model.

MARTHE: What is it?

PAINE: Nothin'.

She collects her bag. Lotte croons a German song at the front door. Marthe turns her back on her in the doorway to the hall.

MARTHE: If it's fear for your manuscript weighs you down ...

PAINE: It isn't.

They look at each other in silence. Lotte croons on.

MARTHE: *(Low voiced)* I cannot help that I am reared for righteousness, Mr Paine ...

PAINE: *(Low, fierce)* ... You married a **catholic**, Mrs Daley ...

MARTHE: *(Louder)* ... And am still barred from Prayer Meeting two years after his death, for my sins.

Lotte stops singing. Fireworks go up in the almost dark of the day, flaming their faces.

PAINE: *(Distinct)* Love is sin?

LOTTE: *(Calling)* Momma.

MARTHE: *(Eyes still on his)* Hier, liebchen.

She shakes her head very slowly, blocked. Leaves. Paine watches her out. Sits at table: model under its cover; pipe; rum. He removes the cover, reveals an intricate wooden toy bridge arching north to south over a painted wood map of America. The single-span arch has thirteen sections, each bearing the name of a colony delicately painted in. The keystone-section has dislodged. He uncorks the bottle. Picks up the fallen section: Pennsylvania. Slots it back in. Takes a box from his pocket; a polished jet Indian necklet from the box. Lets it fall on the bridge. It dangles, like a rope.

His face.

Terse images of his New Year's Eve:

He stands looking at her bed. On the reverse, we see the model and the necklet on the two pillows, a note on each.

His desk, empty save for bottle, glass, lamp, watch. His hand lifts the glass. He sees his reflection in the window. It pains him.

His cot, lit by held lamp: their presents, two packages, await him on the pillow.

Desk again. A wood-framed portrait of Mr Thomas Paine by Lotte. His hands rip open the second package: a fair copy of "Common Sense" by Marthe, a short note attached. Tears scald his eyes.

53

PAINE: Damn, damn, damn ...

He lies on the dark cot, fully dressed, the almost empty bottle hanging inert from a flopped hand, Marthe's fair copy clutched to his chest. Close shot of the barely visible face. The lips move on soundless words. A sudden spume of fireworks across the sky-light reveals a death-mask face, eyes rolling on dream beneath the shut lids.

PAINE: *(Mumbles from dream)* Yes. No.

A hammering sets up, a fist at the front door.

PAINE: *(Flailing up from sleep; loud)* Yes?

Dim-lit hallway. Fist on door again, a man's voice calling him. Paine arrives shakily.

PAINE: *(Calls)* Wait.

He turns up the dimmed lamp on the wall.

MATLACK: *(From outside)* Come **on**, we gotta get **goin'** boy. *(Paine opens door, Matlack talks right on)* Our printer friend just stepped out of his wig, he told Cannon he means to have changes this night to what ye writ or he don't print. I got the cart here ...

PAINE: ... Wait on, damn the man, what's his problem ...?

MATLACK: ... He've read your damned scribble, **that** be his problem, and it's turned his cods to custard, serious ... There's treason writ on every page, he says ... Best wrap up, s'colder'n a witch's tit. *(His eyes have suddenly glazed past Paine towards the back of the house)* Aw shit, man,

Matlack recedes; Paine frowns, closes door, dwells, turns. Sees Marthe in the scullery doorway, her hair down for washing, a cloth to dry it in her hands.

MARTHE: Ye'd best go.

PAINE: Ye came back.

MARTHE: Ye were snoring.

PAINE: Stewed.

Silence. He sees the jet necklet at her throat.

PAINE: Looks well.

MARTHE: *(Touching it)* Do it? I never wore such a thing.

He holds up the fair copy, still held in his hand.

PAINE: This *(Shakes head)* I have no words for this ...

He gathers his topcoat reluctantly from a peg, struggles it on.

PAINE: An hour, not more. *(She says nothing)* If ye would sleep ...

MARTHE: Leave that. *(He looks at the fair copy, still in his hand; shakes his head; wants it with him.)* Go do your business.

He nods, tucks it inside his coat, leaves. She watches.

Bell's house and printshop in Southwark. Night. Matlack's brewery cart stands outside the printshop. Two militia stand on picket duty by the door, muskets at the slope. Light from a lantern flares within, as the three inside approach the street. A gathering sense the place is being watched. Bell shakes hands with Paine and Matlack, hugging Paine's manuscript to his chest. The militiamen do their version of a salute as the two head for the brewery cart. Paine winks, deadpan, at Matlack; Matlack starts to chuckle.

City Streets, midnight. Matlack rushes the brewery cart through the hard-rut streets, laughing demonically, slowing for nothing, neither people nor patches of freezing fog. Paine hangs on for his life. The bells of the city's seventeen churches ring in the New Year. Germans fire muskets in the air, shouting and hallooing; scatter as the cart ploughs through them. Fireworks arc and pop in the chill sky. Unnoticed, a handsome coach-and-four ripples silkily in their wake for several blocks, Matlack pushes his drays, the coach falls back into the fog.

Paine indicates a dropping point, Matlack reins in. The fog's thicker.

MATLACK: By God, ye lie like the devil, Tom Paine, where'd ye get all that fancy patter from ...?

PAINE: Wasn't the patter won him, Tim, was the promise of a bigger slice o' the pie.

Paine clambers down. The coach-and-four silks past, stops by an alleyway half a block ahead. The Brewery drays shy as it passes, Matlack tidies them up.

MATLACK: They bin smellin' mare since we set off, must be onea them buggers ...

He points to the barely visible coach ahead. Several cloaked men have alighted, melt into the fog.

PAINE: *(Reaching up for handshake)* Thank ye, friend.

Matlack winks. Clatters off. Paine lifts Marthe's fair copy to his nostrils. Sets off for Walnut, two blocks ahead. Passes the still stationary coach. The coach begins to follow at the walk, draws level.

MAN'S VOICE: Mr Paine, is it?

Paine peers at the shadowed figure within.

PAINE: *(Still on the move)* Who asks?

MAN: *(Languid; arrogant ruling class English)* John Anderson, your servant, sir. I'm given to understand ye've been scribbling treason against the Crown. Be so good as to hand it me, sir, and we'll let the matter rest.

Paine stops. The coach holds. Anderson's gloved hand reaches out to receive the manuscript. A firework screams high above them; explodes a flood of weird red light across the pair. For several beats the man's smiling face is clearly there: Captain John Bully Anderson's.

PAINE: Ye spy for the Crown, is that it?

MAN: *(Cane-head to roof)* I bid ye bye bye, Mr Paine.

The coach pulls calmly away. The firework dies. Paine shivers, clutches the fair copy to his chest. A small sound drags his head up. Three men stare in silence at him, paces away; they're dressed as Iroquois braves, their faces crudely corked, clubs in their hands. One shows pot teeth in a grin.

POT TEETH: *(Harsh Cockney)* . Bye bye, Mr bloody
   Thomas traitor Paine.

A sound from behind. He swings round with a shout. Sound of his body hitting the ground; the fair copy spills from his nerveless hand. A corked hand reaches in to gather it.

Marthe's sitting room, *night. Mantel clock ticks on the silence: gone two. Marthe sits in her bedrobe, reading her Bible. A parcel of drunks slide down the street outside, headed home: goodnights, good tidings. A rap on the window, a thud on the door. Marthe lays her book down, glances at clock, a humouring smile on her face. Removes her wedding-band, lays it on the table, heads for the front door. We stay with the ring.*

MARTHE: *(En route - voice lifted)* Stewed again, is it, Mr
   Paine? *(Another thud on door)* Nay, nay, I shall open in
   my time, not in ...

Sound of Paine, falling into the hall; her scream.

Bedroom. *Paine's battered face on the pillow. A man's thumb lifts an eyelid, lets it fall.*

DOCTOR'S VOICE: The bones'll mend, Mrs Daley, but the
   cold's brought up an old fever in him we'll have to
   watch. Feed him if he'll take it, keep him warm ...

Bedroom. Early daylight. Marthe carries a stove in, lays it by the bed, kneels beside it to pray. Paine mutters. She looks up.

PAINE: Cold.

MARTHE: Oh God. Oh God.

PAINE: Cold.

Sweat burns from his barely recognisable face. She stands. Removes her robe. Enters the bed beside him. Draws him to her. Hugs him like a child.

PAINE: Cold, mama.

Fade sound.

Print workers' voices, laying up, preparing for the pull.

Bell's printshop. *Day. A press: a slow deliberate pull: a title page:* **Common Sense on Independence**

PAINE'S WRITING VOICE: The sun never shone on a cause of greater worth ...

Tailor's shop. *Close up, styled sequence of an undisclosed man being fitted with breeches, coat, stock, stockings, shoes. The tailor ducks and weaves around him. Lotte and Will watch with interest from a corner of the room.*

PAINE'S WRITING VOICE: ... Tis not the affair of a city, a country, a province, or a kingdom, but of a continent - of at least one-eighth part of the habitable globe. Tis not the concern of a day, a year or an age; posterity are virtually involved in the contest, and will be more or less affected even to the end of time, by the proceedings now ...

In a final mirror reveal, we see Paine reviewing his reflection, nose crinkled with diffidence.

PAINE'S WRITING VOICE: ... O ye that love mankind, ye that dare oppose not only the tyranny but the tyrant, stand forth to receive the fugitive and prepare in time an asylum for humanity ...

The tailor offers a wig. Paine shakes his head, face pale, a bit scarred; recovered.

LOTTE: Is he gonna be a king ...?

WILL: Uhunh. Gonna be a gen'l'm'n ...

PAINE: *(Finished)* Come on, you two, fall in, we're goin' places.

The State House Yard. Spring day. Paine, Lotte and Will cross the Yard. A town marshall touches his hat respectfully as Paine approaches the building. A town crier calls out the latest war news: "British Armies headed for New York. General Washington draws up American defences." Paine gathers a broadsheet from him as he enters the House.

*State House Corridors. Paine reads the war news broadsheet as the kids scout ahead, searching for the door. A placard indicates **Congress Offices** ahead. Lotte points at one. Paine nods; knocks.*

PAINE: Now you people comport yerselves in here. This here's Congress. Clear?

The kids nod. A secretary answers, Paine gives his name, the man recedes. They wait.

LOTTE: *(Wriggling, holding her stomach)* I wanna go.

PAINE: Oh God, Lotte ...

WILL: Me too.

Jefferson, tall, sandy-haired, arrives in the doorway.

JEFFERSON: *(Virginian)* Mr Paine, this is indeed an honour, sir. Thomas Jefferson.

PAINE: *(Taking his hand)* Aye, how do. D'ye have a necessary, my companions are caught short ...?

JEFFERSON: *(Unphased)* We do indeed. Come ...

He leads them into the office, details the secretary to deal with it, the kids follow him through a connecting door, Paine takes the proferred chair, fiddles a little with the tight, unaccustomed breeches.

JEFFERSON: Your daughter, is it ...?

PAINE: No no, just a pair of friends.

*Jefferson smiles, resumes his seat at the desk. Lifts up an open copy of **Common Sense** he's been working from. Paine takes it in.*

59

JEFFERSON: This is a remarkable piece, sir.

PAINE: Thank ye. It's not bad.

JEFFERSON: General Washington has commended it to all his staff. Sam Adams is handing out free copies across Massachusetts. Ben Franklin believes it to be a work of genius, and is probably even now reading it aloud to the King of France. *(Paine chuckles; Jefferson joins in)* Says it's made this fight for independence possible, recruits are flocking in. I hear not even the Bible sells as well, is it right?

PAINE: *(Plain)* Well, there's talk of a hundred and fifty thousand by year's end ...

JEFFERSON: *(Whistles)* And how does it feel to wake up one morning a man of fortune?

PAINE: Best ask the publisher. I signed my share to Congress, for the war. Ye know Mr Franklin?

JEFFERSON: *(Quietly)* Not well. But enough to love him, I believe.

Paine nods. Relaxes. Warms to the man. The clerk returns the kids to the room, sets them on chairs by the window overlooking the Yard.

JEFFERSON: May I speak in confidence, Mr Paine? *(Paine nods)* Two days ago, in secret session, Congress moved to set up a small committee to examine and report back upon one of your book's key proposals.

PAINE: Go on.

JEFFERSON: I now head that committee ... charged to draw up a ... Manifesto, I believe you call it ... for the Independence of America.

Long silence.

PAINE: Oh boy.

JEFFERSON: It occurred to me, since ye've been so active in promoting the notion, ye might be willing -

informally, of course - to lend a hand with the declaration that will inscribe it.

He smiles. Paine's eyes have moved to the window, where Lotte is doing her Queen of England act out on the balcony.

PAINE: Hey, sit still, ye beggar ...

Lotte frowns, displeased. Will grins. Lotte spits at him. Will frowns, spits back.

PAINE: *(On his feet)* ... Ye'll excuse me, I'm going to have to get these wee monkeys home ...

JEFFERSON: *(Standing with him)* Of course. Ye'll think on it?

PAINE: How long do we have to get it writ?

JEFFERSON: A week. Not more.

PAINE: *(On his feet)* Sounds about right. For a Declaration of Independence, I can give ye a week.

They shake hands. Paine beckons the kids to join him. Puts an arm round each.

PAINE: One thing I'd say, Mr Jefferson. No declaration will be worth the ink and paper that does not rid these shores of slavery forever.

JEFFERSON: I know it, Mr Paine. Though whether my colleagues will be persuaded ...

PAINE: ... They better, sir. Or it'll come back to burn 'em ...

Paine ushers the kids from the room; waves from the doorway. Jefferson smiles; makes a note in his book.

Recruiting Centre. *Day. Jim Cannon's up on a table, drumming up volunteers. A small crowd has gathered to hear him. The better classes hurry by in a wide, veering arc. Paine arrives with the two children, stands briefly at the back to listen; gives Cannon and Matlack a wave; stares down at the leaflet someone has thrust into his* *hand, sends the kids home with a coin each; studies the notice in his hand. In his point of view, the leaflet, bearing Washington's name, calling for volunteers for a Flying Column to help the Northern Army.*

Marthe's scullery, *mid-evening. Light fading fast. Lamp-lit, Marthe works her dough at the table for tomorrow's loaves. A small tap-tap at the window. Another. She looks up, tugged from thought. Sees Paine at the window, half-melded in her own reflection. It takes a moment or two to realise he's in uniform.*

Marthe's bedroom. Evening. Lotte plays with a doll and the model bridge; they're taking a stroll from Massachusetts to Virginia, across the wooden map of America. Below, voices lift and fall away, stressed, unhappy, anger-flecked. She stops the game for a moment to listen, face grave.

MARTHE'S VOICE: See it, you'll be killing people from my homeland ...

PAINE'S VOICE: ... If they fight for the British, they must take what's coming ...

LOTTE: *(Calling)* Momma! **Momma**!

Voices cut below.

MARTHE: *(From foot of stairs)* Sleep, liebchen.

LOTTE: Your shouting wakes me, momma.

Marthe looks back at Paine, hunched in a chair, head in hands, in the sitting-room she's just left.

MARTHE: *(Softly, from hall)* All right, liebchen. See. I'm quiet.

She stands a moment, listening. Paine looks up at her. She returns to the doorway briefly.

MARTHE: *(Calm; bleak)* Do what ye will. Perhaps it is right ye go. Perhaps it is wrong ye stay.

She moves to the scullery, turns up the lamp, begins filling a bowl with rainwater, lays by pumice, a slice of soap, preparing a body-wash. Paine follows eventually; watches from the doorway.

PAINE: ... Sixty days is all ...

MARTHE: *(Withdrawn into process)* Go. 'Tis settled.

PAINE: Love, I helped start this thing, this ... chance to change the world. Can I now preen myself while others ...?

MARTHE: ... Die? Say it.

PAINE: I cannot call up war from a chair and let some other poor bugger fight it, Marthe. And I ain't gonna die. 'S a promise.

MARTHE: *(Low; fierce)* Ha.

PAINE: What?

MARTHE: I'll hear no more promises, Mr Paine. Take your life, do with it what ye will. It is not my affair.

She washes her legs with cloth and soap. He watches her hand move beneath the skirt, to thigh, to groin; half turns away, his back against the passage wall.

MARTHE: *(Relentless)* The good Lord spoke at year's end, I shut my ears on Him and took your battered body to my bed ... God will not bless this godless union, there's an end on't. My world is old, ye have no place in it.

She washes on. He listens from behind closed eyes to her cloth scouring her flesh.

PAINE: An' if I love ye ...?

The cloth pauses. Silence. Scours on.

Paine's bedroom. Night. A fat moon framed in a skylight. Paine lies propped on his bed, staring at it. A sound draws his eyes to the doorway: Marthe's there, wraith-like in her bedrobe, watching him.

MARTHE: Hold me. Oh God, hold me.

His arms open for her, she moves to fill them; their bodies bind on the tiny cot, senses answering what sense can't. Love and fear and hurt, indistinct, urgent, mutter up from the bed, but their mouths are on other things. The moon glows on, indifferent.

Sound fades. Bring up:

PAINE'S WRITING VOICE: When, in the course of human events, it becomes necessary for one people to dissolve the political bonds that have connected them with another ...

Countryside*. Morning. A plump sun, rising. Paine rides north across the hazy roll of New Jersey. The proclamation continues:*

PAINE'S WRITING VOICE: ... a decent respect to the opinions of mankind requires that they should declare the causes which impel them to the separation ...

New Jersey*. Day. Fog. Images of the dwindling army's long slogging retreat down New Jersey. Bare bloody feet sink into iced mud. Cannonades burst ahead, behind, above the pathetic daze of part-time soldiery. Paine trudges with the rest, eyes flinted over, face mudspecked. The white-horsed Washington rides remorselessly on, face clenched, eyes unwavering, his own icon, ready for Rushmore.*

JEFFERSON'S VOICE: ... We hold these truths to be self-evident, that all men are created equal, that they are endowed by their Creator with certain unalienable rights ...

Fog still. The crushed army huddles on the New Jersey bank, waiting to cross the Delaware. Flat-boats poled into position, dodging the steady pulse of ice-floes clotting and surging around them.

JEFFERSON'S VOICE: ... That among these are life, liberty and the pursuit of happiness.

Camp at Fort Lee, 1776. *Late afternoon. A thin winter sun lights a sodden glade of trees. A makeshift team of caulkers out from Philadelphia work hard repairing the banked flatboats. Elsewhere, the men of the volunteer army sit or lie exhausted, dead-eyed. Paine sits by the river, facing New Jersey, a drum cushioned between his legs, paper spread across its head, a quiver of wooden pens across his shoulders, inkpot fastened to his overcoat, deep in a new piece. Light from the dipping sun dapples his page. Mouth mutters to mittened hand, both buried in process.*

The page darkens suddenly. He frowns, looks up and right. A silent horseman towers above him, the sun behind him, haloing the head, the face erased.

PAINE: Oblige me, sir. You take my light.

The rider shucks his horse a pace or two on, stops again with his back to the river. Paine eases to his feet.

PAINE: Excuse me, General. Couldn't see ye there ...

WASHINGTON: May I join ye, sir?

Paine nods. Washington dismounts, ties his horse, finds a place to squat beneath the tree.

PAINE: Take a mug, will ye?

Washington looks at the coffee bubbling on Paine's fire.

WASHINGTON: I will indeed.

Paine deals him a mug. The two men sit in silence for a moment as they drink. Washington's drained, eyes bloodied with fatigue; his hands shake a little as he lifts the mug.

WASHINGTON: Forgive me, Mr Paine. I'd've called on ye sooner, I had not realised ye were with us ...

PAINE: Well, guess ye've had plenty on your plate, General ...

Washington gazes at him blankly. Nods. Silence. Glances at the drumhead.

WASHINGTON: Old Common Sense, eh. Mmm.

PAINE: Ain't so old.

WASHINGTON: Catch a ball, that'll be as old as ye're gonna get. *(Paine smiles. Washington frowns)* Working something up fer us, are ye?

PAINE: Tryin'.

WASHINGTON: What ye call it?

PAINE: Crisis.

WASHINGTON: Mm. Sounds about right.

A harmonica sets up in the glade behind them: a slowed, haunted rendering of 'The World Turned Upside Down'. Across the Delaware, perched on a low ridge, a detachment of enemy outriders in Hessian green keep silent watch on them, ghosts in the mist. Washington picks at his teeth with a tiny twig: Paine catches a glimpse of the polished hickory dentures.

WASHINGTON: Ye gonna say we can win?

PAINE: *(Shakes his head)* Gonna say we will win.

WASHINGTON: Well, let's see. Over there, we have twelve thousand German mercenaries holding New Jersey, behind 'em another thirty thousand British regulars, the best drilled, the best equipped, the best led army this world's ever seen. Up there somewhere ... *(The twig points up-river)* ... I have two generals conducting a private war over who's gonna wear my boots, heading two armies they make damned sure I won't see hide nor hair of. Down there ... *(He points down river)* a terrified populace screaming I should defend Philadelphia and a horrified Congress already upped 'n' offed to Baltimore. Behind ... *(Long pause)* ... five thousand sick and wounded, a thousand fighting regulars, and four thousand green militia scheduled to terminate at year's end and already dreaming of home. *(He sniffs. Blows on his hands)* I scent the game's

pretty near up, Mr Paine. Figure there's but one more
hand to play. And, if we're gonna win, I'm gonna need
some decent cards.

Paine reaches for the pot, pours them more coffee.

PAINE: Aye, I heared ye were cookin' something ...
(Washington looks at him keenly, eyes tight) ... Watched
a weasel run before a hound once till the mutt dropped
from exhaustion. Weasel turned, trotted back, bit the
mutt's cods off. Like he'd planned it all along.
(Silence. The sun's almost gone) I'll have this writ,
pressed and back inside a week, if it's of help. *(He
looks at the ice-packed river)* Hate to miss the boat
though.

*Washington stands, untethers the horse, swings up into the
saddle, barely there now in the gloom. Glances across the
river at the still stationary Hessians.*

WASHINGTON: Five days is all I can offer, Mr Paine. Won't
be no use after Christmas Eve. My boys surely could
do with some cheerin' though ...

PAINE: Five days it is, General.

*He's gone. Paine relights his pipe, reaches an oil-lamp
from a sack, lights it, slings it from a branch to light his
page; resumes.*

Country road. *Day. Snow-loaded, gun-metal sky. Paine
rides a country road, headed for Philadelphia; moves
through a thin trickle of people, carriages, carts, shallops,
a few on foot, abandoning the city.*

Philadelphia. Aitken's premises. *Afternoon. Paine crosses
to the bookstore, a saddle-bag in his hand. Glances en route
at the deserted printroom, the presses covered in sacking.*

*The store's empty. Paine scans the familiar room; finds
Aitken eventually, in topcoat and mittens, staring vacantly
at the stove. He looks old, a touch desperate. Paine taps
at the glass. Smiles. Holds up a sheaf of pages from the
saddle-bag. Aitken frowns.*

Aitken's printshop. Night. Paine works in his old office, the presses drive on below. He checks pages, finds errors, sends them back. The rum sinks in the bottle; he mixes more ink, takes a new pen from his quiver. Walks over to the gallery. Below, the printroom is a blaze of lamps, a dozen or more women - print workers' wives, mothers, children - improvise supplies of food and drink around the space.

Joseph, militia uniform, lays up. The giant journeyman, militia too, already pulling a title page; Aitken supervises, energised by the work: tiny moments of a singular war effort.

Joseph smiles up at Paine; indicates the child at his wife Sarah's breast. Paine nods, warmed.

PAINE: What ye call him?

JOSEPH: *(A grin)* Jane.

Early morning. Paine sleeps on his greatcoat in a corner of the office. Aitken lays a tied bundle of made-up pamphlets on the saddle-bag; a single copy over Paine's face. He wakes. Sits. Stares at the piece. Looks up at Aitken.

AITKEN: So. Ye had it right all the time, Mr Paine.

PAINE: I'll see you're paid for all this, Mr Aitken ...

AITKEN: Yer horse is fed and watered. On yer way, friend ...

Walnut Street. Early morning. Deserted. Paine sits on his horse, staring at Marthe's still, silent house. Kicks on; away.

Countryside. Day. Scuds of snow lash the road he rides, half asleep in the saddle. Calls ahead, glimpses of movement. He jerks awake, alert at once. Begins to pass a long foot column of volunteers, heads down against the driving snow. Arrives at the head. Matlack leads the column, on an 18-hand New Jersey dray he still manages to make look small.

MATLACK: *(Calling)* Tell 'em to hold the boat, will ye, Mr Paine?

PAINE: That I will, Captain.

He waves; canters on.

Command tent, banks of the Delaware. *Night.*
Washington sits at a table in his private quarters, Paine's pamphlet almost read; in an outer section, his general staff and field officers work flat out on details of the planned surprise attack, tracing routes on several different maps of the area, assigning units and materiel. The 19 year old James Monroe, Lieutenant, fetches and carries for the senior men. Paine stands watching, swaying a little with fatigue, waiting for Washington's response.

Washington emerges from his sanctum. His eyes well with tears; he clears his nose.

PAINE: Will it do, General?

WASHINGTON: *(Eventually)* It will do, sir.

Paine nods. Leaves the tent. Washington swings round to the maps.

WASHINGTON: Now, gentlemen. Show me Trenton ...

Bring up a man's voice, reading quietly in open air:

MAN'S VOICE: ... Tyranny, like hell, is not easily conquered; yet we have this consolation with us, that the harder the conflict, the more glorious the triumph ...

Mix to

The banks of the Delaware. *Midnight. Paine sleeps untidily in the back of a haycart, as the reading is taken up by different voices in turn, speaking quietly at different speeds, in different accents, with varying degrees of facility. We track through Washington's assembled rag-taggle army, hearing **The American Crisis** being read aloud by officers or noncoms, company by company, by the banks of the Delaware. Lanterns bob and lift across the throng to light*

*the spoken words. The white-horse general walks before the
lines from end to end and back again.*

VOICE 1: These are the times that try men's souls. The
summer soldier and the sunshine patriot will, in this
crisis, shrink from the service of their country ...

VOICE 2: ... but he that stands it **now** deserves the love and
thanks of man and woman ...

VOICE 3: ... Tis surprising to see how rapidly a panic will
sometimes run thro' a country ...

VOICE 4: ... yet panics in some cases have their uses; they
produce as much good as hurt ...

VOICE 5: ... But their peculiar advantage is that they bring
things and men to light, which might otherwise have
lain undiscovered ...

VOICE 6: ... The same remark may be made on General
Washington, for the character fits him. There is a
natural firmness in some minds which cannot be
unlocked by trifles, but which, when unlocked,
discovers a cabinet of fortitude ...

*Slow mix to reveal the silent crossing of the ice-packed
Delaware, Washington at the prow of the lead flat-boat,
caped, wind-whipped, resolute. Paine's voice takes up the
readings; they pulse on, immingle with the march and the
subsequent engagement. The crossing has taken all of six
hours: it's almost dawn. 2,400 men and 18 guns snail the
treacherous eight miles to the tiny town. Snow joins the
vicious wind, grows to blizzard.*

*The army splits, the sky lightening: General Sullivan
takes the south approach, Washington the north. A
Hessian guard-post on the north edge is taken out in total
silence. The rag-bag army seeps on, Matlack and the
Philadelphia volunteers along with the rest.*

PAINE'S VOICE: ... Wisdom is not the purchase of a day ... I
call not upon a few, but upon all: not on **this** state or
that state, but on every state ...

70

Washington, on high ground, eyes on his watch. He raises a hand, drops it. The two armies launch a synchronized attack on the sleeping enemy. Half dressed Hessians hurtle into the narrow streets with muskets and cannon, attempt defensive action; others simply run off by the thousand. Washington watches; swivels to take in a large enemy detachment fled into an apple orchard, beginning a counter-attack. A Hessian band plays bedraggled martial music. The rag-bags march straight through them, uncowed, undeflectable. Matlack takes a ball in the cheek, spins to his knees, bellows, comes upright at once, drives on.

PAINE'S VOICE: ... Up and help us; lay your shoulders to the wheel ... Let it be told to the future world, that in the depth of winter, when nothing but hope and virtue could survive ... The city and the country, alarmed at the common danger, came forth to meet and to repulse it ...

Washington spurs his horse down the hill, cloak flapping, sword raised, issuing boyish victory whoops as he comes. Below, a thousand enemy stand hands on heads in surrender, weapons discarded. The Americans eye each other inquiringly along the line: did we do it? Was it us?

PAINE'S VOICE: It matters not where you live, or what rank of life ye hold, the evil or the blessing will reach you all. The far and the near, the home counties and the back, the rich and the poor, will suffer or rejoice alike ...

Washington arrives. The rag-bags begin a low-throat roaring welcome: Hessian officers are brought down their lines, to the tune of The World Turned Upside Down. The voices fade on the still, dank air.

Mix through, eventually, to the haycart back on the Delaware camp-site, Paine asleep on it under his greatcoat.

Close shot of his sleeping face. Noon. A wood-pigeon burbles overhead. He wakens suddenly, blinks for the bird, lifts himself to his knees, scans the deserted camp over the side of the cart, checks the empty jetty.

PAINE: God **damn**. *(He stands, picks up his musket, throws it back into the hay)* Missed the goddam boat, can ye believe that? *(Kicks the cart-side)* God damn.

Church bells, spry, joyful. A pastor's voice giving thanks to the Lord for the victory at Trenton.

Trenton. December, 1776. *Day. Washington and Paine share the front pew of the packed church. The General sits with head bowed, deep in prayer. Paine has his arms loosely folded, watches him.*

Lt. Monroe sits close to the General, his right arm slung, neck and shoulder bandaged. Scan of the crowded pews behind them, hale, halt and lame crammed in to give thanks. The crowd spreads to each wall and back to the porch; flows out into a huge overspill in the freezing yard and streets.

The service ending in song. Washington and Paine leave first, watched by the silent soldiery. In the porch, they reach for their pegged greatcoats: Paine's has gone.

PAINE: I'll be damned. Robbed in a church of God, that's rich ...

WASHINGTON: Here. I have another.

Paine takes the coat, looks at it, is touched.

PAINE: Nay, it'll never fit ...

WASHINGTON: *(Simple)* It'll fit.

They leave the church side by side: a great roar greets them; God bless the General, God bless old Common Sense. A pipe band strikes up: "The World Turned Upside Down" in spry march time.

Washington's carriage. *They have a window each, acknowledging the applause and calls of greeting from the dense crowd of citizens and soldiers.*

Paine catches sight of Matlack, towering over the rest.

PAINE: *(Calling)* How is it, Mr Matlack?

Matlack turns his head to show him: the musket-ball has blown a great hole in his cheek.

MATLACK: *(With difficulty)* Coulda bin worse, friend. Coulda took my cods off ...

Paine waves. Saddens. Sits back in the carriage, eyes closed. Washington looks across at him.

WASHINGTON: Best if you take those down, Mr Paine ... *(He indicates the General's insignia on the greatcoat shoulders)* ... unless ye're after my boots too, with all the others ...

Paine looks at the great barge-like boots; shakes his head.

WASHINGTON: ... Perhaps my triumph here will keep 'em quiet for a while ...

He returns to the crowd. Paine looks at him carefully, sniffing ego, vanity, career in the man, unsettled by it.

Paine turns away; scans the crowd again: the plain folk of Trenton, for a while hopeful again. His eyes are drawn to a little family group: a fair-haired mother, her arm round her twelve year old son; a Quaker father, bearing their Lotte-like daughter on his shoulders. The carriage slows for a corner; the father calls something, Paine hasn't heard, cups his ear for it.

FATHER: *(Hat in hand)* I say: I pray for peace in our time, Mr Paine ...

PAINE: *(Quiet; indicating the daughter)* I pray for peace in hers, sir.

Long shot of the almost royal procession through the crowded streets. A slow pulse of heads being bared as the great pass by.

WASHINGTON'S VOICE FROM THE CARRIAGE: Congress turned down my plans to take ye on as my Press

73

Officer. They have other ideas for ye. A Treaty
Conference with the Indians over at Easton.Then
something in the Capital. If ye're agreeable.

Philadelphia. State House. *Paine waits in an antechamber, his gear piled up around him on the floor.
Closed double doors, men's voices rising and falling
behind them, indicate a full Congress in session.*

*The double doors clack open, Sam Adams hobbles out to
meet him. A handshake, a frown at Paine's Indian garb
and gear: steeple hat with a single eagle feather, bone
necklets, armlets, painted bark masks, amulets, wampum ...*

SAM ADAMS: Ah yes, ye've been treating with the Indians,
reckon they'll hold to their word?

PAINE: I reckon, Mr Adams. While we hold to ours.
They're Americans too ...

SAM ADAMS: *(A nod; pressed)* Secretary to the Committee
for Foreign Affairs, carries a hundred a year, how's that
sound? *(He waits. Paine says nothing.)* Ye do good
work, Mr Paine, Army Recruitment up fifty per cent
since your *Crisis* paper. *(Smiles, liking him)* I can hold
it for a week, let me know ...

Begins leaving.

PAINE: Wouldn't stop me writing on the war, would it?

SAM ADAMS: Write what ye want, friend. *(Dry)* It's sort of
the idea ...

*A flinty smile; the wan old man hurries laboriously off.
Paine watches him head for a door marked Necessary.
The Chamber doors clack open again, the meeting's
broken, Members move out en route for their lunch.
Several Southern members - Laurens, Henry, Richard
Henry Lee - smile approvingly as they pass; a clutch of
Northerners - John Jay, Robert Morris and Gouverneur
Morris of the pantomime wooden leg - regard him coolly.
Paine watches the self-important figures a moment, then*

dips again to begin regathering his baggage. Hears the chamber doors clack open behind him.

JEFFERSON: *(On the approach)* May I help ye, sir? *(Paine turns precariously, arms filled)* As I live and breathe, the great man himself ...

PAINE: Great men don't carry their own baggage, Mr Jefferson.

JEFFERSON: Quite so, sir. *(Claps his hands, beckons a house servant by outer door)* Will we take a bite together?

PAINE: Uhunh. I need to get home.

Jefferson regards him carefully, studying the choice of word. The house servant joins them.

JEFFERSON: See these are taken below, would ye, please? And stand my carriage by for Mr Paine, there's a good fellow ...

Paine drops the gear in a heap, relieved to be shot of it. Jefferson takes his arm, leads him out to the staircase. Stops at the rail, looking down on the hum of Congress delegates conniving and caucusing below. They stand side by side, stare down on the moil. Gouverneur Morris and Robert Morris, deep in business.

JEFFERSON: Did ye speak with Sam Adams?

PAINE: Aye.

JEFFERSON: Did ye say yes?

PAINE: Not quite. I have the feeling somebody may be tryin' to use me ...

JEFFERSON: What here? In Congress? I'm amazed. *(Paine gives a low chuckle, liking him again)* If ye take it, ye've but one task, Mr Paine: to ensure ye let no-one muzzle ye. This has grown a poor place for seekin' the truth in ...

PAINE: I'll see what I can do.

He begins to head for the stairway, calls back as he goes.

PAINE: The Declaration, sir. Not a word on slavery.

JEFFERSON: I did what I could, Mr Paine. They struck it out.

PAINE: *(Shaking head)* It'll be back.

He heads on for the house servant waiting with his gear by the front doors. Jefferson watches, as the weirdly garbed Paine threads through Congress like a man from another planet.

Marthe's house on Walnut Street. *Jefferson's limo stands outside; the African driver smokes a pipe. Paine deposits the last of his gear by the door, returns to the carriage. Hands him a scrap of paper.*

PAINE: Call at this place for me, will ye? If there's a boy there, bring him over.

The African touches his hat, clicks off. Paine returns to house, gazes in at empty sitting room, moves to the back.

Marthe's house, the scullery. Marthe, on her knees, scrubs the tiny floor. Stops suddenly. Sees him staring at her through the narrow window. He tries to smile at her; can't. She's immobilized, caught inside contradictory feelings. Stands. Motions him in.

PAINE: *(Doorway)* Didn't die.

MARTHE: I prayed ye'd live. *(He wants to close with her. She holds up her gleaming hands, looks for a cloth, to prevent it)* Go through ...

He skirts the wet floor to the passage. She dries her hands. Palms her hair. Locates her wedding-band. Returns it to her finger.

He stands in the sitting room, takes in the simple homely order of the place, face pale, nervy, uncertain how things will be. Copies of 'Common Sense', 'Crisis I', 'Crisis II' on the mantelshelf: Lotte's drawn his picture on each of them, a long gangling stick of a man, but recognisably

Paine. He clocks an unfamiliar small metal trunk in the corner. Marthe in, glass of cider on a tray.

MARTHE: *(Laying it by window chair, brief stare at street)* Was that your carriage I heard ...?

He watches her avoid him, take her own seat by the fireplace, the space defined between them; sits, back to the window, to face her.

PAINE: Aye, I used a carriage. Is Lotte here?

MARTHE: Out. She's walking.

PAINE: Took longer than I thought. *(She says nothing, twists the wedding-band a little)* Did ye receive the letters I wrote ye? *(She shakes her head. He frowns.)* Ah.

She reaches for a small inlaid box, opens it with a key, takes out an envelope, slit across the top.

MARTHE: I did receive this, though. From England. Ye'll forgive me for opening it; I saw it was from lawyers and thought it might be a death, the family ...

He crosses, takes it, examines it, frowns at the crude rectangle of missing vellum where the seals had lain.

MARTHE: ... Lotte had the seals, she invented a birthday for the African boy, that was his present.

He returns to his chair. Lays the envelope on his knee.

MARTHE: Ye'll not read it?

PAINE: I can guess what it says. I know the attorneys ...

Silence. The clock stirs to strike the hour.

MARTHE: *(Low; controlled)* Why did ye not tell me?

PAINE: Marthe, what had it to do with us?

MARTHE: *(Releasing)* ... May God forgive ye, Tom Paine, may God forgive us both, ye have a wife and never told me, came to my bed and never told me ye were another's, doubled the sin and damned me, damned me in God's eyes.

PAINE: *(Struggling for control)* ... Marthe, listen, woman. Her father died a debtor, she needed a husband to retain the business, he was a friend, I said yes, there was no marriage, there was a legal ...

MARTHE: ... I don't want this ... In God's eyes we are ...

PAINE: *(Snapping; on his feet)* What eyes? What God? I do not know this God whose eyes never lift above a man's codpiece or a woman's clouts, I do not know this mean-eyed, prying, peeping, prurient monster. My God holds a whole universe in perfect harmony, my God asks justice and truth and love on earth, my God asks only we be useful, do good, make this sty of a world a place fit for his creation to dwell in ... When a man hardens, when a woman softens, what God can it be that scowls and threatens the eternal fire? Not a God at all, a figment dressed by men, and part of the sty **my** God would have us clean ...

The clock strikes: three tinny bangs. He turns away from her, stares out at the still street, angry, blocked, a touch hopeless. Sees his gear piled on the step.

PAINE: I brought ye presents, love.

A shriek from the back of the house, Lotte runs the passage, bursts into his arms, as he stoops to take her.

LOTTE: ... I saw them on the step, I knew, I knew, you're home again, God bless ye Mr Paine ... I done lots more drawings ... Will we read later? Will we?

He hugs her close, eyes closed, his world spinning hopelessly behind the lids.

PAINE: I missed ye, liebchen.

He looks up. A youngish man stands in the doorway, smiling, holding Lotte's cape, just in from the walk.

MARTHE: *(Risen)* This is Mr Gottschalk. Mr Paine.

Paine nods, releasing the kid; standing.

GOTTSCHALK: *(Strong German)* It's pleasure, sir.

PAINE: Aye.

Gottschalk asks Marthe a polite question in German, she answers.

MARTHE: Mr Gottschalk would like to see your drawings, Lotte. Mr Paine may see them later ...

LOTTE: *(of Paine)* Is there a present for me ...?

MARTHE: Genug, Lotte.

Lotte grins, leaves with Gottschalk for upstairs. Paine watches. Sniffs. Looks at Marthe.

MARTHE: Your room is let, Mr Paine. I believe it best for us all it is so. God's will be done.

She leaves, heads back for the scullery. Paine glances out of the window: the carriage has just returned. Follows her as far as the doorway. She kneels where she left off, the implacable work resumed.

PAINE: In a few weeks the city may be threatened again. Keep a bag packed. If ye need to leave, I'll find ye a safe place. *(Pause)* If there's aught ye lack, I'll be at ... I guess, Ma Downey's.

He turns for the front door. Opens it, collects a clutch of Indian gifts, lays them on the stair for Lotte, puts his key on a hall ledge, leaves.

Outside, he stoops for his baggage, sees the carriage heading off down the street,

Will waiting on the sidewalk.

PAINE: Ye feelin' strong, boy?

WILL: Oké.

PAINE: O.K? S'that?

WILL: Mandingo. Means sure.

PAINE: O.K? *(Will nods. They gather his stuff. Paine sits the steeple hat on Will's head; they're off again)* O.K.

PAINE'S VOICE: *(Congress chamber acoustic)* I Thomas Paine do solemnly swear and affirm that I shall faithfully discharge the duties of Secretary to the aforesaid Committee for Foreign Affairs.

State House Committee Room. High Summer. Hubbub, fierce, contentious.

PAINE'S VOICE: ... And shall disclose no matter arising therefrom which said Committee, on behalf of Congress, shall direct me to keep secret. So help me God.

Sam Adams raps table to quell the angry din. The contending sides of the dispute, left and right of the table, glaringly subside.

SAM ADAMS: ... Gentlemen, the motion has been laid. Mr Paine, if ye please ...

PAINE: *(From bottom of table, facing Adams; reading)* "That Congress be advised by this Committee to recall its Agent Silas Deane from France to explain Bills of Lading and Shipment Vouchers recently charged to the Congress by said Agent in the sum of four and one half million French livres."

A handbell sets up in adjacent corridor. Sam Adams frowns.

SAM ADAMS: Those favouring? *(John Adams, Patrick Henry, Richard Henry Lee show)* Those opposed? *(Gouverneur Morris, John Jay, Robert Morris)* Chair says Aye, motion carried. Other business, gentlemen ...?

The handbell draws closer.

GOUVERNEUR MORRIS: *(Getting to his foot)* I shall fight this, I give warning. This is turned into a witch-hunt, not just against Mr Deane, but against the merchant-class itself ... *(Glares at Paine)* prosecuted by persons unable to distinguish corrupt dealings from honest profit ...

John Jay and Robert Morris rap the table in support.

SAM ADAMS: Hearing set for December, gentlemen. To be held in private.

Paine frowns a look at the Chairman. A fist at the door. Mr Buck, Head House Servant, appears, bell in hand.

BUCK: ... Beg pardon, gen'l'men, President wants to see y'all right away in the Chamber, word's in the British've put down a whole army at Chesapeake Bay ...

SAM ADAMS: Thank ye, Mr Buck. Meeting adjourned.

The table has risen, the room already emptying. Paine watches Jay, Robert Morris and Gouverneur Morris exchange dark murmurs. Sam Adams slowly gathers his papers; nods at something cousin John mutters in his ear.

SAM ADAMS: *(Left with Paine)* Looks like a spell in the back-country, Mr Paine. Ye'll gather our effects an' bring 'em on, will ye? *(Paine nods)* Ye think this Deane's corrupt?

PAINE: Ye've seen the files ...

SAM ADAMS: If this gets out, we could see the country split top to bottom ...

He turns, shuffles out. Paine sniffs. Mr Buck reappears in the doorway, checking they've left.

BUCK: Chesapeake's no more than a week's march away, Mr Paine, I'll need y'r stuff on the carts by Friday ...

Paine nods. Mr Buck leaves. The bell sounds out again in the cavernous passageway.

PAINE: *(Letter voice over)* ... Tomorrow or the day after, I believe, will be the latest time ye may leave the city in safety ...

State House. Committee Room Balcony. *Paine stares down on Congress members mustering to board their carriages in the bustling yard.*

PAINE: *(Letter voice)* I enclose a bill to help meet expenses ... My ... warmest greetings to Lotte. (Long pause) And to yourself.

Foreign Affairs Committee Room. *Table laden with tea-chests of files, documents, effects. Paine supervises the house servants removing them. The wall calendar's at 12th September. A clock's booming five.*

Connecting ante-room. Office. *Almost bare. Paine writes at his desk, engrossed. Shouts, sounds of horseman arriving in the yard, draw him out to the Committee Room balcony. Matlack's dismounting, calling news to the House servants loading a solitary shallop with tea-chests.*

PAINE: *(Calling)* That you, Captain?

MATLACK: *(Full beard covering ravaged cheek)* God damn, are you still here, boy? City's at their mercy, Washington's routed, Brandywine Creek ... For God's sake don't get caught, Tom Paine. You they will definitely hang. *(Begins saddling new mount)* See ye in the back-country ...

Paine waves, moves back into the Committee Room. Mr Buck bustles in, ready for the road.

BUCK: That's yer lot, Mr Paine. Shallop's loaded, your horse is standing by ...

PAINE: Leave him ready, Mr Buck, I'll finish up and come after ye ... There's been no callers for me, has there ... a lady ...?

BUCK: Town's nigh on empty, Mr Paine. Only fools left ...

Paine returns to his bare office. Checks his own watch, lays it on the desk, stares at Lotte's framed portrait of him on the wall. Takes it down, stuffs it in his satchel. Resumes his chair. Uncovers the file he is working on. We read: Congress and Corruption: The Case of Silas Deane. Turns several pages of manuscript; dips his pen.

Writes: French Loans for the War Effort.

Night. Lamp; *very low. Paine's watch ticks on the desk: 12.15. Paine scribbles on, a mound of pages already covered. Faint sounds of horses' hooves, a drum, fifes, drawing a touch closer. His eyes blink up suddenly. He listens. Blows out the lamp. Stands by the window. A glint of British cavalry in adjacent street.*

State House Yard. *Paine slings his leather satchel into the shallop, backs the horse into the shafts.*

Market Street. *Night. Deserted. Paine plays hide-and-seek with the British advance party. Noises of occupation increasing. He leaves the shallop in a market-hall alley. Continues on foot.*

Marthe's house, Walnut Street. *Paine rattles the front door of the Daley house, calls 'Marthe' several times, not daring to lift his voice. Cavalry and footsoldiers move through adjacent streets, music louder, more threatening. He sees his letter, pinned to the door. Removes it. A head appears in an upstairs window of the house next door .*

WOMAN: *(Calling down)* Ye lookin' for Mrs Daley, she left a week back ...

PAINE: Know where she went, ma'am?

WOMAN: Nay. Keeps herself to herself, do that one ... Watch yer tail, mister.

The woman closes the window fast, at the sound of soldiers entering Walnut. Paine presses himself against the side-alley wall. The British advance, full martial display, grim, terrifying. Paine's watching face.

Fade to black.

Banks of the Schuykill River. *Winter. Cold, bare, sodden country, sifting rain. Paine rides his horse at a walk along the banks of the river. Ahead, a country inn, an East Indiaman moored at a jetty, several hundred cattle milling around. He picks his way through them, nods to a bonded farm labourer.*

PAINE: *(The cattle)* Where they headed?

LABOURER: City, I guess.

PAINE: The British have the city. They're supplying the
enemy?

*The man shrugs; looks towards the inn. There's a rough
auction in progress under a canvas awning at the rear;
several rich merchants bid for the beasts; a cluster of
farmers look on, glasses of rum in satisfied hands.*

*Paine shucks his horse, heads past them at the walk, eyes
bleak with anger. Rounds the building. A young lieutenant
in the uniform of the Continental Army awaits him by the
front rail.*

LIEUTENANT: Mr Paine, is it?

PAINE: It is.

LIEUTENANT: *(Saluting)* An honour, sir. Lt. Monroe.

PAINE: Aye, ye were at the Delaware. Took a ball in the
shoulder. (A shy nod from the boy) Will he see me?

LIEUTENANT: He will, sir.

Outskirts of Valley Forge. *Late afternoon. The two riders
climb a wooded ridge. Ragged soldiers hack at trees as
they pass. Calls go up from small cooking-fires:* **'No
meat. No meat. Get your fire-cake, no meat.'**

*Paine, taking it in, some yards behind the young
lieutenant. A sudden cannonade from beyond the crest of
the ridge sends him ducking for cover. The lieutenant
reins in, laughing.*

MONROE: Nay, sir, it's celebration ... Ye haven't heard?
The Northern Army took Burgoyne and 6,000 men at
Saratoga, coupla days back ...

PAINE: ... Are ye tickling me, mister?

MONROE: It's fact, sir. God's honour.

They crest the ridge. Look down on the desperate tented

84

camp-site, farmhouses, burnt-out forge. Another cannonade puffs up from below. A small parade of soldiers, midgets at this distance, present arms. Paine halts his horse. Removes his hat; moved.

MONROE'S VOICE: To His Excellency, the General, on his birthday.

Farmhouse. *Night. Washington's HQ and living quarters. Voices echo Monroe's toast. A small private celebration: Washington heads the table, his wife Martha Custis opposite him, Paine to her right, a man in full Prussian uniform to her left, a youth (Lafayette) in full French uniform, arm in sling, next to him, the 18 year old Monroe on the General's left. The toast is drunk, seats resumed. A lull in proceedings, as an aide appears with tomorrow's orders for the General to sign. An orderly hovers, topping up. Paine takes in the table; frowns then grins as he sees Lafayette casually lifting souvenirs from the table and slipping them into his sling. Washington, finished, rises slowly. Takes in the table with grave eyes, face flushed with wine.*

WASHINGTON: Mr Monroe, I thank ye, sir. And I'll call another. To our dear friends from the Old World. To the Marquis de Lafayette, a boy still in years but a man in spirit and a lion in resolve. To the Baron von Steuben, sent I have no doubt by the Great Drill-Master in the sky, to turn my rag-taggle boys into a disciplined fighting force. *(A beat. The General's eyes warm)* To Thomas Paine, old Common Sense himself, whose pen is worth a thousand muskets and will prevail. *(The two men exchange a look)* They are - and it is my toast - the flower of Europe, and I bless 'em.

All rise save Paine, Von Steuben and Lafayette. Washington drinks deep, eyes troubled, a bit desperate. Lafayette stands to raise his glass as all sit.

LAFAYETTE: *(strongly accented)* The peoples of the Old World salute you, sir. For what happens here affects the whole of suffering humanity. On victory here depends

the future of all who look for Liberty, Equality, Justice
and Peace. You lead not only an Army, General
George. You lead a world. *(Glass up)* General George!

*All rise save Washington. The quaint toast is repeated. A
salt cellar falls from Lafayette's sling. Paine grins at
Washington.*

*Night. Paine and Washington sit by the fire; an orderly
refills their brandy glasses, recedes. Silence. Washington
hums snatches of a doleful tune, inturned, a cold anger
working on something. Paine watches him over his glass;
begins to take out notebook and Deane Report from
satchel. Mrs Washington stops in, kisses the General on
his hair, motherly; he pats her hand, fond, remote. She
leaves for bed.*

WASHINGTON: Do ye have a wife, Mr Paine? *(Paine
frowns; shakes his head)* Mm. Man needs a wife.
*(Paine lights his pipe. Washington hums again; gulps
his brandy.)* Those documents on yer knee there, are
they the corruption affair ye're come for my thoughts
on ...? *(Paine begins to open the file)* No no, keep it
shut, I got enemies enough in Congress without
stickin' my nose in their private chamber pots, as we
speak there are elements in that esteemed body plotting
with my fellow generals to have me removed, oh yes,
keep it shut, sir, I may not be drawn on this matter ...
(Paine closes the file. Sniffs.) My advice to you would
be much the same. Speculation, peculation and an
insatiable thirst for self-enrichment may well have got
the better of every other consideration in many of our
countrymen, but you lift yer head up to speak it, Mr
Paine, ye'll catch a ball. In the meanwhile, you 'n'
me's got a war to win. That's the crisis.

*He drains his glass, lays his head back, eyes closed.
Paine looks at him; pushes notes and file back into his
satchel; lays down his glass, moves to the window, stares
out at the high ridge in hard moonlight. Snow has fallen,
shimmering the earth. Sentries call, answer, on the hill.*

PAINE: With respect, General, the crisis ain't only the War or the Army any more. The crisis is everywhere and everyone. Why we fight. What world we would put up in place o' the one we bury. A nation born in greed and graft and corruption will surely drown in them. Same as a Congress allowing these lawbreakers to prosper will lead us into private anarchy and public squalor. Which is to say, just another form of tyranny ...

A log falls, sputters, on the hearth. Paine turns his eyes back into the room. Washington dozes, his mouth open, wooden teeth bared, brandy glass precariously still to hand. Paine watches a moment, eyes sombre; crosses to finger the glass from his hand; pads carefully from the room. Washington snores softly on.

Valley Forge, *morning. Snow on the ground. Tents still in use, but the shapes of cabins have begun to spring up, men swarming about them, sweating in the cold sun. Two wagon-loads of young volunteers from France, just arrived, draw cheers from watching Americans.*

Paine riding through at the walk, on his way, Washington's greatcoat tail draping his horse's rump. Lafayette struggles up level with him, hurrying to welcome the French.

LAFAYETTE: Frenchmen, Mr Paine. Answering the call. And there'll be more ... even our King supports ye, as I hear it ...

PAINE: Good to know it, sir ... (Looks down at his sweating face) And what'll ye do when it's over, all this ...?

LAFAYETTE: I'll take the good news back home, sir, and see it's put to use ...

He peels away, free arm raised in salute to the young volunteers. Paine shucks the horse forward and away, Lafayette's flowery welcome to the troops in his ears. Passes Von Steuben drilling a company of regulars in German, French, Dutch and some bits of English, his command of the vernacular to say the least uncertain, his hard voice arcing over the assembled men's merriment.

VON STEUBEN: *(Screams)* Goddam sacré bleu, yankee scheisse buggerluggers ...

The site covers two miles: Paine passes a whole world; an irregular army being licked into shape. A sentry gives him a salute. Paine looks down at him: he's barefooted, stands in his hat for relief.

SENTRY: *(Shouts)* See ye back in Philadelphia, Mr Paine? We'll have the buggers driven out come Spring.

PAINE: *(A wave)* You bet.

Paine nudges his horse along the edge of a creek, the camp almost done. Ahead a ways, camp-followers wash clothing and utensils in the iced water. He reins left to avoid them, heading for trees. A woman calls from the creek.

WOMAN: *(Calls)* What, too risen in the world to know old friends, is it, Mr Paine?

He turns the horse. A young woman has approached from the water, hands wet and raw with cold. He stares hard at her, uncertain. She grins.

PAINE: My God, it's little Philly ...

He swings down, she moves forward, hugs him, for a moment his daughter again.

PAINE: What in heaven're ye doin' here, girl ...?

PHILLY: Married a soldier up in New York, didn't I, he took a ball at Fort Washington, I'm back doin' what I do best till somefin' better turns up. I heared ye was put up with the General. *(He nods)* Better'n livin' in the shit wi' the rest of us, eh?

PAINE: *(Bringing wallet out)* Listen, I have something for ye ... *(She watches him work out a wad of bills)* ... Here ...

She takes the notes. Examines them.

PHILLY: What, ye wanna jump'r somein'?

PAINE: That's the three weeks rent ye left me, plus interest plus depreciation, near as I can make out ... *(She holds the notes up in turn, examining them)* Something wrong?

PHILLY: See. *(She hands him a bill)* See ... *(Another)* Philadelphia's spelt wrong ...

PAINE: *(Looking)* No, that's how it's spelled ...

PHILLY: So I bin told. That's how ye know it's counterfeit. The true ones have it wrong, see ...

He takes a real one, holds it up: Philadelphia's spelt "Philadelpkia".

PAINE: I'm damned.

PHILLY: Let's hope the buggers makin' 'em are as well, eh?

She hands him several more. He replaces them. She tucks the wad in her sleeve.

PHILLY: Glad I seen ye, Mr Paine.

PAINE: Aye. *(He wants to say more; can't find what it is)* Thank ye for what ye did ... back there.

She holds her hand up, wiggles the fingers.

PHILLY: One good turn, eh ...? Fat lotta use this'd've been in my line o' work but fer you ...

He smiles. Remounts. Stares at the frail waif-like woman below. Shakes his head. Rides off. She watches unperturbed, her own person somehow, despite the shit.

Fade to black.

Fade up sound of military pipes and drums: "The World Turned Upside Down".

The streets of Philadelphia. *Summer. Washington leads the army in solemn repossession of the capital city. Crowds stand sullenly to watch. Glimpses of burnt, boarded-up buildings, refuse and excrement everywhere, ravages of a brutal occupation.*

The army passes. A long line of Congress carriages follows. Hats return to heads, hisses, boos, calls greet the returning delegates. Sam Adams' face, stony; others.

A file of shallops and carts bring up the rear, carrying Congress effects. Paine rides his horse in their midst, scans faces for Marthe and Lotte, finds only sunken eyes, sullen mouths, hunger, resentment. Cuts left up Walnut, leaving the procession.

Walnut Street. *Paine approaches on foot, skirts a large crowd of women hammering at the locked doors of a grain warehouse. Glimpses a fearful merchant behind an upstairs window, pistol in hand.*

Rear of Daley house. *He passes the canvas awning. Stops, eyes widening, fear-flecked. A man, woman and two sons are moving furniture inside. The sons look at him warily; the father appears, a chair in his hand.*

PAINE: The Daleys have gone?

MAN: Aye. Sold and left.

PAINE: Is there ... an address? *(The man frowns)* I'm a friend.

The man fiddles a piece of paper from his trouser pocket, hands it to him. Paine looks at it for several moments. Hands it back.

PAINE: I'm obliged.

MAN: Ye'll remember it?

PAINE: Aye.

Mrs Downey's boarding house. *Paine lugs his gear up the narrow stairway, lays it down in his old room. Places his globe by Will's which wears the feathered steeple hat. Touches the feather. Goes down the stair again. Mrs Downey serves rum to a group of Continental Army regulars in the saloon.*

PAINE: Boy around, Mrs Downey?

Mrs Downey turns, a frown on her face.

MRS DOWNEY: No, he ain't.

PAINE: Ye know where he is?

MRS DOWNEY: Ye could try the Common ... *(Paine nods)* The British took him just 'fore they left . Caught the poor starvin' mite wi' half a loaf in his hands ...

Paine stares at her blankly. Blinks, whitefaced.

Paine running the Common, eyes fixed on something ahead in the distance.

A stand of English oaks on the mound, bodies swinging by the neck from each. A Continental Army cart works methodically along the line, cutting them down and carting the bodies.

Paine's face, on the run.

PAINE: *(Through teeth)* No, no, no.

Slows, on the approach, falters, stops. Walks slowly forward.

His point of view up and ahead, past the working soldiers, to Will's swollen face. Wind tugs the body, for a moment gives it life. The sign around his neck becomes readable:
THIEF

Paine closes on the body. Puts his arms around the bound legs. Pushes his face into the lad's knees.

SOLDIER: Hey up, mister, we'll have him down in a tick fer ye, losin' him's cost ye a few bucks, eh, I'll bet ... No better than heathens themselves, the bastard British ...

Paine holds on, lost. The soldier's bayonet severs the rope, the kid falls across him like a sack. He stands there, motionless; nowhere to go. Sound fades.

Fade to black.

Fade up sounds of women's voices demanding Bread and Justice.

State House Yard. Paine crosses the yard. Several hundred angry people, most of them women, in town meeting, bunched around a group of Philadelphia Assemblymen addressing them from a large electioneering cart, festooned with posters and placards. Assemblyman Matlack's huge voice calls for people's committees to regulate essential food prices and investigate profiteering rackets. Assemblyman Rittenhouse, beside him on the cart, gives Paine a nod.

Paine heads on for the entrance; looks up as he goes; sees Gouverneur Morris on the Committee Room balcony, staring down at him.

Committee Room. Paine arriving, face gaunt, wintry. Gouverneur Morris turns, re-enters the room, closes windows.

GOUVERNEUR MORRIS: Come in, Paine, take a seat.

Paine squints a frown at the empty room, sits, the length of the long table between them.

GOUVERNEUR MORRIS: *(Taking Report from his satchel)* I trust you're recovered from your illness. *(Paine nods)* The Committee has asked me to thank you for the work you have given to this Silas Deane Report. However, it is my duty to inform you ...

PAINE: *(Quiet)* Where's Sam Adams ...?

GOUVERNEUR MORRIS: *(Implacable)* ... that after due deliberation the Committee has decided to place this Report on the table *sine die* and to terminate all investigations and proceedings into the doings of Mr. Deane. *(Stares up at Paine)* Do I have your word this is the sole copy ...? *(Paine nods)* Good. *(He stows the Report into his satchel, locks it, levers himself upright, begins to clump out past the still seated Paine, stops by his shoulder to hand him an envelope.)* In there you will find a copy of the oath you swore to keep secret whatsoever this committee shall instruct you to keep secret. You are so instructed. For the wellbeing of our country, we intend to bury this affair in respectful silence ...

He clumps on.

PAINE: I thought Sam Adams had the chair here ...

GOUVERNEUR MORRIS: Governance is once again back in the hands of men of sound character and unclouded mind. Ye'll excuse me, I have important matters to attend ...

He's gone. Paine sits on, dealing with it. Opens the envelope. Stares at the handwritten oath. In the Yard below, a woman's voice calls for Bread and Justice.

Mrs Downey's boarding house. *Paine's room. Night. Globes, steeple hat, feather, Lotte's framed picture, desk, files, vouchers, a sheaf of manuscripts in Paine's writing, pen, ink.*

Paine face down on the bed, staring at the wall. A light knock on the door. Ignored. Another. The door pushes open: Jefferson. Paine looks at him, struggles slowly to sit, an unshaven mess.

JEFFERSON: What's this, Mr Paine? Gone to ground?

Paine gives him a wan smile. Waves him to the desk chair. Runs a hand through his wild hair.

PAINE: What brings ye to town?

JEFFERSON: Your letter. *(Paine nods, warmed)* In these times, an honest man has a hard job finding company. *(Looks at the manuscripts on the desk)* Ye've been busy. *(Reads)* ... "While the poor and middling of this land are in desperation for their daily wants, this corrupt creature Deane will be allowed to skim a quarter of a million of their taxes on a claim I have proved and Congress knows to be fraudulent ..." Mm. Is it finished?

PAINE: All but.

JEFFERSON: And what then?

PAINE: They have me hog-tied, these strutting grandees of Congress, who turn their backs on the poor and powerless and run this country like a god-damn **business** ... *(He holds, on the edge)* What would you have me do, Thomas? They aim to bury this thing. In silence.

Jefferson stands; takes in the tiny room, touches the eagle feather, hands Paine the rolled copy of the Philadelphia Packet he's been carrying.

JEFFERSON: Spoke with the Editor on my way over. He can't wait to read it. *(He tips his hat. Begins to leave)* Do what you do best, Thomas. Make a din.

Paine opens the Packet, thinks it through. We catch odd items: the War; Food Riots during the Christmas season ...

State House. *Antechamber/Congress Assembly Room. Bitter voices rail behind the closed double doors to the Chamber. Paine stands very still, watching them, face pale, composed; fishes a sealed envelope from his coat pocket, ensuring it's there. The doors bang open. The Serjeant of the House ushers the protesting Press Corps from the Chamber.*

HOUSE STEWARD: *(Calls)* House in closed session. Mr Thomas Paine to the bar, if ye please.

Paine enters the tense, crowded, now silent chamber. Gouverneur Morris sits at the President's table, flanked by John Jay and Robert Morris. Flashes of others: Sam Adams, Jefferson ...

GOUVERNEUR MORRIS: *(Packet in hand)* Here is a paper of December 29th. In it is a piece entitled 'Common Sense to the Public on Mr Deane's Affairs'. The President is directed by Congress to ask if you are the author?

PAINE: I am.

GOUVERNEUR MORRIS: Very well. You will be informed of our judgement. You may withdraw.

Silence.

PAINE: Judgement? What's the charge?

GOUVERNEUR MORRIS: You may withdraw, Mr Paine.

PAINE: I'm to be tried but not heard? Are we now a
tyranny again?

Gouverneur Morris clumps to his foot, snorting.

GOUVERNEUR MORRIS: Ye've broken your oath as a servant
of this House ... and it is as a servant that you shall be
treated. I will not be lectured to on democracy by a
mere adventurer from England, without fortune,
without family or connexions and ... *(A glance at the
Packet)* - as far as I can make out - without grammar ...

His supporters hoot their glee. Sam Adams rises, calls
Shame on ye, *the Morris claque shout him down. Paine's
face, taking it all in.*

GOUVERNEUR MORRIS: Ye will leave this chamber at once,
Mr Paine, or I will ask the Serjeant to throw you out ...

*More din. Jefferson rises to protest Paine's treatment, is
shouted down. Paine takes out the envelope, lays it on
the ledge before him.*

PAINE: ... I'm a man of peace, mister, but I shall leave this
chamber on my own two feet and only when I'm
done ... *(The din subsides. He scans the Chamber.)* An
Agent of this Congress asks a fortune in commission
on a transaction which he claims to have been a loan
but which all in this House know to have been a gift to
the American cause from the King of France. This
House, for whatever reason, has shown itself ready to
lie to the people to cover the fraud. Gentlemen, there
are some of us who set out in '76 to found the best
place on earth, the first great, good, just nation. This
House, it would seem, has turned its back on that ideal,
preferring but another private corporation to promote
the interests of the already rich and powerful. I cannot

offer allegiance to such a House and such a paltry notion. *(To Morris)* You have my resignation, sir.

He turns, leaves.

GOUVERNEUR MORRIS: ... This House will decide how your contract will be terminated, Mr Paine ...

PAINE: *(Over shoulder)* This House may do what it will. sir. I no longer serve it ...

Track him out, face gaunt with stress, tension. The doors boom to behind him. He stands for a moment, breathing deep, distressed, rather wild, somewhere between laughter and weeping. Voices lift again behind him. He walks away from them.

Common Graveyard. *Winter. Paine stands at a tiny plot, staring down at a rough headstone. We see crudely carved, the words* **Will Okay**. *Wind cuts through grass, bare branches.*

He turns away; David Rittenhouse and his daughters wait for him on the path. He joins them. Fragments of their talk, as they leave the yard.

They stop by the gate.

RITTENHOUSE: What'll ye do?

PAINE: *(Headshake)* I don't know, friend. Feels like the end of something.

Rittenhouse nods, looks at his daughters waiting down the lane, hands Paine a box he carries in his hand.

RITTENHOUSE: I hear ye have a birthday coming.

A handshake. Rittenhouse joins his kids. Paine stares down at the box; opens it; takes out a perfectly constructed compass; opens the cover: Newton's universe shimmers on its face. Closes cover again. It's a Rittenhouse.

Country lane. *Early Spring, Pennsylvania. Paine rides his gear-laden horse down a back-country lane. Asks* *directions of a passing farmer on a cart. Crests a rolling hill. Ahead, a small farmhouse nuzzling a thin river.*

PAINE'S WRITING VOICE: The times that tried men's souls are over ...

Later. Paine, still mounted, watching something in the distance from beneath a large oak.

PAINE'S WRITING VOICE: ... And as the scenes of war are closed, and every man preparing for home and happier times ... I take my leave of the subject.

His point of view: a fair-haired woman and young daughter wash bed-linen at the stream. Paine reaches out his telescope. Lifts it to his eye. Telescope view of the two: Marthe, Lotte, Marthe again. He lowers the 'scope, returns it to its case, perhaps preparing himself to head down to them.

A shout from the farmhouse. A man appears, carrying a large basket. Lotte runs to meet him; he nuzzles her hair fondly.

Paine watches a moment longer; reins the horse round; heads back up the hill.

WASHINGTON'S LETTER VOICE: My dear Paine, I am presently put up not far from Princeton and not very far from where I am informed you currently lodge. It would give me some pleasure to have you as guest here, if you are free and willing. Apart from all else, your presence here may remind Congress of your past services to this country. By one who entertains a lively sense of the importance of your works, George Washington.

Large Mansion, Rocky Hill. *Conservatory. Day. Washington sits in a huge, throne-like chair, in Roman toga and crowned by a golden laurel-wreath, having his portrait painted. Monroe arrives in the doorway.*

MONROE: Mr Paine's arrived, your Excellency.

WASHINGTON: Is he there, show him in, will ye ... *(Paine steps forward - his version of spruce - in borrowed clothes)* Mr Paine, welcome, welcome, sir.

PAINE: *(taking him in)* Good to see ye, General.

WASHINGTON: Ye have a room? Good. The college here have commissioned a portrait ... *(plucks at the toga)* ... not my idea these, I do assure ye, but be at home, there's a gaggle of Congress folk staying, they're in the library I believe ... Try not ... antagonizing, would ye ... *(Paine nods, a thin smile)* ... Oh, and I've spoken with Robert Morris about your wants, he's about somewhere, it might pay ye to have a word ...

PAINE: I'm obliged, sir.

WASHINGTON: We won a war, Mr Paine.

PAINE: We did, Mr Washington.

He leaves. The emperor returns to his pose, chin lifted, profile secure, eyes on posterity.

Mansion Dining Room. *Night. Supper over, the ladies retired. A servant serves port at table, another offers cigars. John Jay, Gouverneur Morris and a young James Madison fill one side; Robert Morris faces them on the other. Washington's chair is empty. Paine lights his clay pipe at the fire, resumes a seat at the bottom of the table.*

GOUVERNEUR MORRIS: Not heard much from ye in recent times, Paine. Keeping occupied, are ye?

PAINE: Aye, you could say so.

GOUVERNEUR MORRIS: What, writing?

PAINE: *(mild, factual)* This and that. *(small pause)* Been working on my grammar. *(another pause)* Spent a lot of time scanning the public presses, waiting to catch a whiff of apology from the erstwhile champions and defenders of the now celebrated British agent, Mr Silas Deane.

Silence. Robert Morris chuckles through cigar smoke.

ROBERT MORRIS: Well, it's pretty clear you've lost none of your talent for saying the right thing at the wrong time, mister.

The doors open, Monroe in.

MONROE: The general will be with ye presently, gentlemen, there's a problem with the breeches ...

ROBERT MORRIS: ... Or his belly.

Washington arrives, spooned into a magnificent new uniform. Applause from the table as he returns to stand by his chair.

WASHINGTON: Forgive me, gentlemen, but if I'm to wear it at my farewell next Saturday, I shall need to break the devil in beforehand ...

He lowers himself carefully to his chair, as the suit's admired around the table.

JAY: I hear your army had plans to set ye up as King of America, General ...

WASHINGTON: ... Till I scotched 'em, aye.

GOUVERNEUR MORRIS: I suspect the country would have welcomed it, sir. I certainly shouldn't have minded. Men need someone to look up to. It's human nature ...

WASHINGTON: ... Ye may be right, but it won't be me, sir. I have a farm and a family I've barely seen in eight years ...

ROBERT MORRIS: Oh, ye'll be back, sir.

WASHINGTON: No no ...

ROBERT MORRIS: Well. We shall see.

Silence. And odd uneasy sense that Robert Morris has gone too far, or too near, for comfort.

WASHINGTON: And what about you, Mr Paine? What'll ye do in the peace?

PAINE: I'm building a bridge.

WASHINGTON: You're building a bridge?

PAINE: Aye. In cast iron. Single span, big enough to cover the Schuykill, the Hudson, the Thames even ...

ROBERT MORRIS: I'm damned.

PAINE: Looking for capital to develop it.

ROBERT MORRIS: Good on ye, sir. Ye'll have to tell me more, it's possible I can help ye.

PAINE: I'll do that.

JAY: Does this herald your farewell to public life, Mr Paine, along with the General here ...?

PAINE: It's possible, Mr Jay. I wouldn't bank on it. *(A glance up the table at Washington)* I wouldn't bank on either.

Washington signals more port, leans forward to send Monroe on an errand.

WASHINGTON: Ye know what I would enjoy, gentlemen? I would greatly enjoy a reading from his work by America's greatest author ...

ROBERT MORRIS: Capital!

MADISON: Yes indeed.

Grunts from Gouverneur Morris, John Jay.

WASHINGTON: I would not want Congress or the people to forget the debt we owe him ...

GOUVERNEUR MORRIS: I think it unlikely the gentleman will readily fade from memory, sir ...

WASHINGTON: *(easy)* Save your irony, sir ... There is a saying in Virginia ye may not have in New York: never offend a king or a writer. Each has the power to make you sorry, Mr Morris ... *(to Paine)* What d'ye say? Will Common Sense read Common Sense?

Monroe returns with a package.

PAINE: I have no copy.

WASHINGTON: Hand it to Mr Paine, if ye would. *(Monroe lays the package on the table before Paine)* Remember the British spy I hanged a couple of years back, André he called himself, real name Anderson? *(Paine nods)* I found that package in his possession. I believe it's yours, sir.

*Paine opens the package carefully, face pale, taut. Reveals Marthe's fair copy manuscript of **Common Sense**, her New Year's note still attached: "for Mr Paine, May '76 be the future he writes for, in friendship, Marthe."*

WASHINGTON: Come, sir, ye'll not refuse us.

Paine blinks. Flicks across the pages. Finds the passage.

PAINE: *(reading)* ... But where, say some, is the King of America? I'll tell you, friend, he reigns above, and doth not make havoc of mankind like the Royal Brute of Great Britain. Yet that we may not appear to be defective even in earthly honours, let a day be solemnly set apart for proclaiming the charter; let it be brought forth placed on the divine law, the Word of God; let a crown be placed thereon, by which the world may know, that so far as we approve of monarch, that in America the law is king. For as in absolute governments the king is law, so in free countries the law ought to be king and there ought to be no other. But lest any ill-use should afterwards arise, let the crown at the conclusion of the ceremony be demolished and scattered among the people whose right it is ...

Silence for a longish time. Paine stares at Marthe's note.

New York. *Assembly. The New York Assembly Speaker, reading bill awarding Paine a farm in New Rochelle for his services to America.*

The Speaker's voice continues, over, as Paine rides north, across green land, under an uncertain sky.

New Rochelle. Small farmhouse. Paine approaches. A family - farmer, wife, three children - sit out on the porch, busy at chores. They watch Paine arriving.

PAINE: Good day to ye, I'm Mr Paine.

FARMER: Aye, heared ye was comin'. I'm Mr Lees, Mrs Lees there, them's the kids. *(Paine raises his hat to them)* You wantin' us out?

PAINE: Not that I know.

FARMER: You raisin' the rent?

PAINE: What is it?

FARMER: Hundred a year.

PAINE: Sounds about right. Mind if I look around?

FARMER: Your farm, mister. Heared the State o' New York give it ye for services rendered, s'that right?

PAINE: Aye.

FARMER: What did ye do?

PAINE: Oh ... a bit o' writing.

FARMER: Hunh. Writin', eh? *(a small grin)* Guess that beats workin', any day of the week.

Paine grins, tips his hat, rides off across the meadows.

SLOW FADE TO BLACK.

FADE UP DOCK SOUNDS.

New York Docks, 1787. *A line of passengers boarding a ship for Europe.*

Close shot of Paine: he's fifty, a touch thicker in the hip but lean still, blue eyes still fierce. His eyes scan the quayside, watching for someone to show.

Wives and children kiss husbands good-bye. Carriages bustle in, more Passengers decanted. Paine finishes the scan. Picks up his leather satchel. Heads for the gangway.

Pauses to watch a group of French army war-maimed being helped to the ship. Removes hat to mark his respect.

His name's called from down the quay. He turns, sees two men trotting a sedan chair towards him, bring it to a halt beside the gangway.

Ben Franklin lumbers slowly from the chair. He's eighty, heavy, far from well, shine enough left in his eyes. He carries a dozen or so letters in a bundle.

FRANKLIN: Here, take these, letters of introduction to men of influence ...

PAINE: Ye should be in bed, Mr Franklin.

FRANKLIN: Bed's for births and deaths, sir. I'm past both. Ye go to England now? *(Paine nods)* And ye'll go to France, yes? *(Paine nods again)* There's a letter there for Lafayette, make sure ye see him, I hear he's grown important ...

PAINE: ... I will, I will ...

FRANKLIN: ... And watch out for those damned genders. I've had trouble from genders all my life, I wager I'd still find the French feminines a plague ...

They chuckle together for a moment. A handshake.

FRANKLIN: Damn ye, Tom Paine. You're going to miss my funeral.

Paine shakes his head, gazes at the old man's frail face.

PAINE: Ye think we'll let ye die? Ben Franklin? Uhunh.

He picks up his satchel again, heads up the gang-way, turns as he reaches the file of boarding passengers. The roll call sets up on deck. Franklin still watches him.

PAINE: The wig, sir. *(Points to his head)*

FRANKLIN: The wig? What's wrong with it?

PAINE: I'm no expert, but I'd say ye'd got it about face ...

Franklin feels it. Frowns.

FRANKLIN: Does it show?

PAINE: Ye have to look close.

He goes. Franklin pulls the wig off with a flourish. His balding head gleams in the sun.

FRANKLIN: *(Calling)* That better?

Paine turns. Nods. Grins. Disappears. Franklin hobbles back to the sedan.

From above we hear his name called: 'Thomas Paine.'

And, eventually, his "Aye".

FADE SOUND.

FADE TO BLACK.

INTERMISSION

FRANKLIN'S VOICE: ... If there be one certain problem with the certain prospect of dying, it is that one is forced to spend a certain amount of time considering one's Maker ...

PHILADELPHIA, 1790. Franklin's bedchamber. Loose profile shot of Ben Franklin propped in his fourposter sick bed, speaking to empty room, his wig hung from one of the posts.

He turns, looks for the lens; the shot tightens; he smiles, finding it.

FRANKLIN: *(81; ready for off)* ... But you know something? We only die when we fail to take root in others. And that's probably the only afterlife we're like to have, whatever the churchmen say. Living on is living in. So. Where was I? Paine, yes of course ... Went back. Left home to go home. Few understood why. Planning an iron bridge, he said. Visit his folks before they died ... Mebbe. Or mebbe it was just that nose of his. Maybe he smelt something back in that king-ridden class-riddled midden we call Europe. And who's to say he's wrong, now that the French have followed our example and brought their divine rulers to their knees, kings, lords, cardinals ... the whole sorry Pantomime of MisRule in those parts ...

He turns his head to the door; sees his son-in-law, Mr Bache, hovering in the doorway, scanning the room for sign of a listening other.

FRANKLIN: *(Abruptly)* I've been dwelling on Paine a little, Mr Bache ...

BACHE: *(Alarmed)* Pain, sir? I'll have the doctor fetched at ...

FRANKLIN: **Thomas** Paine. My friend. Bugger still owes me thirty pounds.

BACHE: *(Muttered)* Can't say it surprises me, father-in-law, he was ever a ruffian ...

Franklin fixes him with a rheumy stare.

FRANKLIN: *(Flinty)* An empty bag never stood upright, Mr Bache, as I believe I remarked on your betrothal to my daughter. Are they gathered?

BACHE: *(Squirming)* They are, sir, yes.

FRANKLIN: Best send 'em up then.

Bache backs uncomfortably out. The old guy lies back, eyes closed. Slow rasping breaths scrape the silence. The room slowly begins to fill with family, three generations, old to infant, covering the space like snow. Some weep, others stare blindly at the parchment face of the corpse-to-be. Silence. Franklin's eyes open, first one, then the other; take in the throng.

FRANKLIN: What a grand surprise. Thought I was in heaven for a moment. *(Tickles the nose of a seven year old great-granddaughter with a finger.)* Thank you for coming to see me off. But if ye'll forgive me for the inconvenience, I've decided to see in the Spring, so shall we say a couple of months? April sounds right. Blossomtime. Come back April ... Mm. Go now, if ye please. Good to see you all. Waiting for news from France, ye see.

He closes his eyes, sets up the heavy breathing again. Bache signals retreat, jaw clenched with irritation, the family sift out to the stairway.

Franklin judges them out, then opens his eyes, finds the camera.

FRANKLIN: News from France? We'll see. *(Thin grin)* Some of us, anyway ...

FRANCE, 1790, Calais Harbour. Winter. Evening. Passengers debark from the ship.

A freshfaced young American, William Short, scans faces anxiously.

Paine appears, in Washington's army topcoat, leather satchel on shoulder. The young American moves nervously forward to greet him.

SHORT: Mr Paine? William Short. Welcome, sir. The Minister's most glad ye agreed to come at such notice ...

PAINE: Ahunh. How far's the inn, I need to put my head near a pillow ...

SHORT: We sleep in the coach, sir. Matters have become more pressing, we leave at once. But I can promise you a pillow, sir. And a blanket.

PAINE: And a bottle, I hope ...

Short smiles, draws rum from his pocket. Carefully opens the door of the coach. Holds out the bottle.

SHORT: Minister's compliments.

Paine sniffs; takes, reads, pockets. Steps past the proferred hand, heaves himself into the coach. Short takes pillow and blanket from the driver, passes them inside to Paine, climbs in to join him.

PAINE: What about yourself, Mr Short?

SHORT: *(Angelic)* I shan't be sleeping, sir.

Paine looks at the freshfaced youth. Short looks shyly back at the veteran, smiles, looks away. The carriage begins to pull away.

PAINE: How old are ye, boy?

SHORT: Twenty three, sir. Well, twenty two ...

Paine fiddles a folded planpaper from his satchel, opens it on his lap: a structural drawing in side-elevation of his bridge-to-be, surtitled "Mr Thomas Paine's Proposed Iron Bridge Over The River Shuykill".

PAINE: Good ages.

Paris, *bridge over the Seine. Carriage, on the move. Paine gazes out, reading the city. The plan still rests on his lap, his scribbles everywhere. Light, airy snores from across the carriage. Paine takes a sup at the bottle, glances across at the sleeping Short, head deep in the pillow, blanketed to the chin. Smiles. Returns his gaze to the city. Winces at something he sees. His view of long stretch of high granite wall. Severed heads on pikes, withered, there for months, float at intervals atop it.*

Coach turns to enter courtyard of large buildings. Above the archway, the US Ministry emblem and the crossed flags of France and America. A crowd of cockaded sailors gather at the coach, study the US seal on the door, converse with the coachman, applaud the two men inside: **Vive l'Amérique! Vive le Président Washington!**

Ministry reception area. *Late afternoon. Paine waits to the side of large ornate double doors, watching a panicky crowd of American merchants and businessmen clamour at a young clerk's desk for exit documents. The doors push open, young Short signals him through.*

Minister's drawing room office. *Late afternoon. Paine moves in through the double doors, takes in the large salle,* *pads down it towards the untenanted desk. Removers and office staff work round him as he goes, removing and crating files, documents, personal effects. A door opens at the bottom of the room: Jefferson smiles out at him, shirtsleeved, waistcoat unbuttoned, hair a mess; waves a greeting. A handshake. They study each other in silence for a moment.*

JEFFERSON: Does the heart good.

PAINE: Aye. Likewise. *(A wave at the removers)* Someone goin' somewhere?

JEFFERSON: *(Taking his arm)* Come through.

He leads Paine through a similar chaos that is his private quarters to an inner sanctum, shuts the door, waves him to a chair, pours wine, hands him a glass. Paine takes in the room. President Washington, in oils above the mantel-piece; a map of Europe on a demonstration easel near the window, a chaos of flags and coloured pins.

JEFFERSON: *(Toast)* Common Sense, I think.

PAINE: *(Glass up)* If ye say so.

They drink to the bottom, like Russians with vodka. Jefferson tops up.

JEFFERSON: And France.

PAINE: And France.

They sip, lay down their glasses. Jefferson studies him, eyes grave, some anger in him.

JEFFERSON: Time's scarce, Tom, here's what's in my mind. I'm called home. Against my will and against my advice. Sail Friday. For the next halfyear, perhaps longer, who knows, the US Ministry to France is to be represented by Willie Short, the green young man who brought ye in, a good and sweet and capable boy, no doubt, but lacking a certain weight, shall we say. My friend, matters here are not as calm nor as ordered as they might be, the violence and rioting of last summer have abated, but what caused them hasn't gone away, there is still no constitution written and enacted, the precarious compact between the King and the Assembly of the Nation begins to wobble, a small step out of place and France could yet be plunged back into last year's carnage ...

PAINE: Aye, I saw the heads on the wall comin' in ...

JEFFERSON: And there'll be more, my friend, unless calm minds and seasoned hearts can prevail. *(Sips, thinks)* Tom, I know ye're a busy man, a bridge to build and the politics of England to attend, but it would help me and our country much if ye would agree to spend time in this place while I'm away ...

PAINE: Doin' what?

JEFFERSON: Anything and everything, meeting the key people, the groups and factions that seethe beneath the surface. Mebbe a book, who knows ...? Ye can tek my word for it, friend, there's books aplenty on the way, all paid for by the crowned enemies of progress ...

PAINE: *(A wintry smile)* Put public life behind me years back. Ain't scribbled in ages ...

JEFFERSON: Look, it's enough you're seen to be here, letting France and her enemies know by your presence America's her friend and sworn to help her revolution prosper through the difficult days ahead. There's a room at White's Hotel for as long as ye want it, ye can use this place for office, my staff have instructions to furnish ye with whatever ye need. What d'ye say?

PAINE: *(Frowning, sucking his lips)* I'll give it thought.

JEFFERSON: There's a Farewell Dinner in my honour this evening, it'd be grand to announce Tom Paine'd be laying his head here for a time while I'm gone. *(Grins)* But please, tek yer time. Never were one fer rushin' in, as I recall, were ye ...

PAINE: *(Chuckle)* This Thomas Paine feller, ye think they'd know who ye meant ...?

JEFFERSON: Common Sense? The philosopher of revolution? Oh yes. Sure of it.

PAINE: *(Gathering his gear)* I need sleep ...

JEFFERSON: Tek my coach, Mr Short'll bring ye there ...

They head for the door; stop at an oil portrait of Ben Franklin on the wall. The old guy beams benignly down on them.

JEFFERSON: He's missed, is he not?

Paine nods; pulls a face at the old rogue. They head through the chaos of outer offices.

JEFFERSON: Present yerself at Lafayette's place en route, if ye will, he's burstin' to see ye.

PAINE: He's big cheese here now, ain't he?

JEFFERSON: None bigger. Heads the National Guard. Holds the balance between King, Assembly and People. And keen to have ye on board.

They reach the outer door. Short appears. Paine and Jefferson shake hands.

JEFFERSON: It's important this, Tom.

PAINE: Aye.

He leaves, no fuss, Short in his tailstream. Jefferson moves to a window, watches Paine emerge into the courtyard and stride towards the carriage. In closer shot, the Minister's face is tense, grave.

The Tuileries.** Lafayette's huge library in the Ducal Palace. Paine waits, for the moment unattended. He takes the place in, wholly undwarfed by it: family portraits, books by the thousand, objets, effortless wealth. A liveried servant lights lamps down the room. Paine crosses to watch. The man lights two nightlights in red glass at a table set behind screens. In slow reveal we see the extraordinary space: Lafayette's shrine to the American Revolution, walls and surfaces bearing tumultuous witness* *to that shaping experience. Swords, State Flags, epaulettes, badges, honours, decorations, framed addresses, letters from Washington and Congress, lists of fallen comrades, all incongruously interspersed with the silver tableware filched from Valley Forge. A large portrait of Washington dominates. Beneath it, copies of Paine's writings in American and French (Common Sense, The Crisis Papers) mounted under glass. By them, at the heart of the shrine, a hand-written copy of the* **Declaration of Independence, under the heading AMERICA; and next to it, under FRANCE, in another hand,* **La Déclaration des Droits de l'Homme et du Citoyen.***

Paine's face, reading the place, living the history, gradually drawn back to the passionate days. His hand moves reflexively to his lapel as he watches; touches the old pen he keeps there.

LAFAYETTE: *(Arriving, on the walk; in goodish English)* ... Mr Paine, back in the fray, I prayed you will come, most welcome, sir. A quite collection, is it not?

PAINE: Indeed. Pleasure to see ye, sir.

A warm handclasp. Lafayette, 30-some now, thickened in trunk and face, continues buttoning his commandant's brilliant tunic, a valet bearing his ceremonial sword in tow.

LAFAYETTE: You will forgive me if I do not stay long with you just now, I am to an audience with the King, your Ambassador Jefferson will be there, affairs of state. You will take supper here, it's arranged, later we talk ...

PAINE: *(Trapped)* Aye. Thank ye.

LAFAYETTE: Ye'll be my guest of course. Ye like this room?

PAINE: *(Nonplussed)* ... I guess.

LAFAYETTE: Take it. Good for writing, I think. *(He tells the servant. Paine studies the portrait of Washington, then Lafayette's identical uniform. Lafayette notices, smiles.)* Exactly, sir. I had it made expressly ...

The servant leaves. Lafayette joins Paine at the shrine.
They look in silence for some moments.

LAFAYETTE: Now the glove is on the other hand, Mr Paine,
it is we who set our feet upon the road to freedom.
(Paine nods. Stares at the flickering collection) Like
America, we too are upon experiments. But unlike you,
our King and the people have agreed to rule together. It
is my honour and my duty to see all's fair between them.
So we will all keep our heads. It is good you are with us,
sir, France has need of your wisdom. À bientôt ...

He bows, heads for the door up the room. Paine watches
him dwindle; might let him go.

PAINE: *(Suddenly, voice floating across the space)*
Marquis, could ye carry a message to Mr Jefferson?

LAFAYETTE: But of course. You need ink ...?

PAINE: No no. Just tell him Yes, if ye will.

LAFAYETTE: Yes?

PAINE: Yes.

Paine's left. Throws his greatcoat over a chaise longue,
kicks off his travel-boots, uncovers a booze cabinet,
selects a rum, carries it to the Louis XV, drops across it,
bottle on chest. Close shot of his face, flickering red in the
light of the shrine; his hand, unbidden, teasing out the
pen from its holder beneath the spread coat's revere.
Footmen bustle in, carrying a bed. Stop at the chaise.
Paine sleeps, bottle in one hand, pen in the other.

Paris, Faubourg St Antoine. *Midwinter. Hard times in a*
tough quarter. Paine trudges over iced cobbles, seeking
direction. Stops at a long line of working-class women
waiting for bread. His French stumbles, they can't make
him out, pass him down the line. A commotion breaks out
at the bakery door, men have begun loading trays of
bread onto a cart, the women surround it, vent their anger
on the men. The baker pleads the bread's for the National

*Assembly, the women couldn't give a shit. A straggle of
National Guard appear, push the women back into line.*

*Paine moves on towards a large government building
ahead.*

Salle de Manège, *Visitors Gallery. Ex-riding school, now
home of the National Assembly. Paine gazes down at the
floor of the Hall. Deputies move in and out of the great
doors to the Chamber, stop to drink coffee, wine, punch at
the large porcelain Bastille-shaped stove in the centre of a
main aisle. The sashed President calls repeatedly for
silence, ushers repeat the call; little attention paid. A
messenger hands the President a note. He bangs the
raised table with his gavel.*

PRESIDENT: Le Roi arrive, Messieurs! Taisez-vous pour le
  Roi!

*Ushers bounce the call around the Hall, Deputies quieten
a touch; Lafayette appears in full pomp at the great
doors, the King on his arm in day-clothes and cockaded,
leads him in calm silence to the podium. A commotion,
cheering, breaks out at the far end of the Hall, as an
ancient man is ushered forward towards the waiting
monarch.*

Short arrives, out of breath, at Paine's side.

PAINE: *(A whisper)* What kept ye, Willie?

SHORT: Sorry, sir, thought I'd found ye someone, but he's
  caught a chill. I believe I've someone for tomorrow
  though ...

PAINE: I need help, Willie. I might as well be in Turkey.
  So, what's goin' on ...?

SHORT: *(Checking Orders of the Day)* That's Jean Jacob, I
  believe, the oldest republican in all France, being
  presented to the king. Says here he was christened ...
  (Squints at the paper) ... can't be right, can it? ... one
  hundred and twenty years ago.

PAINE: *(Smiles, shakes head)* Hmm. Good on the old bugger!

The King hands the ancient a scroll. The old guy takes it, turns to the Deputies, his back to the king, begins singing a frail reedy version of Hoorah for the Cockade. The place explodes in cheers, applause, singing.

Short's antechamber office. *Day. Paine strides in, in a hurry, heading for the Minister's doors.*

PAINE: *(On the move)* Is he arrived?

SHORT: *(On his feet)* Mr Paine, a word if ye ...

PAINE: ... Gather up the English papers for these last weeks, will ye? I need the Parliamentary Reports ...

SHORT: ... Mr Paine, there may be a problem ...

PAINE: *(Disappearing)* ... Later, Willie.

He enters Jefferson's big room, scans it for signs of life. A woman turns from a long window to look at him. Silence; on his face, a dim flicker of an earlier moment: Marthe in Aitken's office. He crosses to the desk. Opens his appointments book. She moves towards him, ignores the chair. She's tall, strong-bodied, pale-haired; twenty-two; confident, direct eyes; speaks easy, idiomatic English; carries a bundle of recently pressed newspapers in her hands.

CARNET: I understand you require assistance with our language?

PAINE: That's right, I'm keen to know this place ...

CARNET: Good. It would be an honour to help you, Paine.

PAINE: Are ye French, Miss ...?

CARNET: Carnet. I am. But my father's Irish. From Dublin. Carney. *(Paine nods)* Is it formal lessons you ask, it's not clear ...?

PAINE: No, I need someone to move around with me, explain what's going on, the Assembly, the Courts, meetings ...

114

CARNET: ... I understand. You plan a work on our Revolution?

PAINE: *(After thought)* It's possible.

CARNET: Good. I think we fall asleep, you'll wake us up ...

PAINE: Ye've read my books?

CARNET: Some. I smuggled Common Sense into convent school under my skirts when I was ten.

PAINE: Ye ticklin' me ...? *(She frowns, serious)* That takes my breath.

A church clock strikes the hour: she looks at the window.

CARNET: Not everyone sleeps, Paine. Last year we rose against the King with three words on our lips and in our hearts. Freedom. Equality. Brotherhood. We're still waiting. Out there, *(A wave at the streets beyond the window)* the poor never sleep.

PAINE: *(Slowly)* I believe ye. And I'd know more.

CARNET: Then you must visit the Political Clubs, the Societies, the people's section meetings, the groups. If you look for the heart, you do not start with the arse.

Silence again. He studies her face. Flicks a page or two in his notebook.

PAINE: So. Not the Assembly, hunh? *(He looks at her. She smiles)* What about the Jacobins, is that ...?

CARNET: Important, yes, but middle-class, large fee keeps 'em exclusive. I couldn't help in any event. No women.

PAINE: *(Turning page)* So. Where would ye ...?

CARNET: *(Decisive)* The Cordeliers. Students, shop-keepers, artisans, workers. Trouser people, the folk who rose last summer. Penny a week admission. Still no women, but it's in our district, I'm known there, there is an arrangement. *(His face asks what)*. Ye'll see if you go.

PAINE: I'll go.

CARNET: Let me know when, I'll meet you. Where d'ye stay?

PAINE: I lodge with Lafayette. The Tuileries ...

CARNET: Mm. Don't get too close, Paine. He will not last.

A silence. She's leaving. Paine's on his feet.

PAINE: I shall need your address ...

CARNET: *(Hands him a newspaper)* ... That's the printshop. We stay above. *(His lips move on the unfamiliar French)* Bouche de Fer. Mouth of Iron. We print weekly.

PAINE: Who's we?

CARNET: *(On her way)* The group who make the paper.

PAINE: Miss Carnet, ye should speak with ...

CARNET: *(Turning)* Carnet. No miss, no mister. I call you Paine. It's better.

PAINE: *(A nod; off-balance but game)* ... Speak with Mr Short about the fee.

CARNET: Are **you** paid, Paine? *(He frowns, shakes his head)* Then we both come free.

She nods goodbye, leaves in a swirl of skirt. Paine scratches his head, bemused. Looks again at the "Bouche de Fer". Crosses to the long window, stares down on the courtyard.

SHORT: *(Doorway; nervous)* Will she do, sir?

Paine watches her thread her way along the crowded cobbles, purposeful, unafraid, offering the paper to those she passes, talking earnestly with those who buy it.

Close shot of Paine gazing down at her, drawn, resistant.

Trail sounds of packed basement.

The Cordeliers Club, *cellars of ancient abbey. Night. Shot of British flag being lit, slowly blossoming to flame.*

Cheers, amused, ribald. A huge long-haired full-bearded German holds it above his head at the Tribune. Paine, watching, unclear what's happening; jots something down in a notebook. The giant German hits his stride: rafts of bad, guttural French push off into the dank, ill-lit, smoke-filled refectory of the one-time Benedictine monastery. Paine again, not at ease, scanning faces, looking for Carnet. The German climaxes, to ironic cheers and good-humoured applause.

CARNET'S VOICE: *(From seat behind, arriving; mouth to his ear)* That's Cloots ... anarchist. Demands an end to all nations, a federation of all peoples, a brotherhood of mankind. He's a Prussian baron, I believe ...

The German leaves the platform, applause sets up again, Paine angles in his seat to look at her; she has on a man's wig over pinned hair, a jacket and britches.

PAINE: This is the arrangement ye spoke of ...?

CARNET: Oui. Is it not ridiculous?

Paine wags his head ironically: not sure. A commotion sets up, people begin chanting a man's name, necks are craned to the doors at the back. Carnet flicks her eyes down the stone-vaulted chamber: Hanriot, the President, a hard man, in sash of office, begins vacating his high-chair.

CARNET: Ah bon. Danton takes the chair for a session, *(A huge bellow from the entrance behind them)* I think he's here ...

DANTON: *(Fort)* Oui, j'arrive, j'arrive.

The din grows. A large unkempt lump of a man strides through the moil, shaking hands, waving to friends, a rolled newspaper in his mitt.

CARNET: *(Over his arrival)* ... Founder of the Club, son of a peasant, lawyer-intellectual, important, I think, brilliant, very daring ...

Close shot of Danton, arriving at the platform: early 30's; broad-boned, ugly, vivid face dark with drink. Hanriot hands him a list, sits by him to applause. Paine, gazing intently; Carnet's mouth at the ready behind him.

Danton climbs the high chair, puts the list on a table. A claqueur fetches a jug of ale, he drinks, ends on a rinsing spit onto the floor, bringing his wig off.

DANTON: *(In French; croaking peasant voice)* ... You gentlemen of the Press will note, please, this is not an intoxicant, I have it from my physician to ease my throat. *(Laughter, applause. He's loved. A man hands him his wig, he slaps it back onto his head)* And I speak at the Jacobin in half an hour, which explains the beaver on my head ...

Laughter rolls about the place; Carnet translates expressionlessly; Paine flicks a stunned say-again glance at her around the word "beaver".

CARNET: *(Sotto; simple)* It means he thinks the Jacobin britches-folk are all cunts.

Paine blinks, turns away. Carnet's translation continues in his ear.

DANTON: Last week we spoke about the revolution. Not as something already achieved, done and dusted. But as something still in the making and still in the balance. To make this revolution real for **all** the people of France, not just the britches-folk and the well-to-do, is now our task and solemn duty. It will not be easy. The lords and bishops, the rich and powerful are still with us, my friends, and will do all they can to return France to their own pockets, where they believe it rightfully belongs. In this endeavour, they will be helped by their brothers and cousins beyond our borders, the crowned and titled and biretta-ed tyrants of Europe, who fear our example will sow the seeds of Liberty in the hearts of their own peoples and threaten their absolute rule. One day, take my word, these monsters will unleash a bloody war against us. For the moment, they are content to open up another front, a war of words and ideas, they wheel out their paid scribes and pensioned hacks to loose the first volleys ... *(Unfurls a London Times in his hand).* Such a one is the erstwhile champion of popular liberties, Edmund Burke, who had this to say in the English Parliament ... I translate: "The French have made their way through the destruction of their country to a bad constitution, when they were absolutely in possession of a good one ... *(Howls of Shame, Liar)* Their Declaration of Rights is no more than an institute and digest of anarchy ..."

The place explodes. Paine's face, still taking translation from Carnet's lips, white with what he's hearing.

DANTON: *(Bellowing above the din)* My friends, now is the time to take the field against these crowned enemies of progress. Now is the time to present our hopes and achievements in words to stir the heart and lift the spirit of the oppressed peoples of all the world ...

He gathers his things to leave, men surge forward to lift him on their shoulders and carry him out. Applause, singing: Ça Ira.

Paine's on his feet, face tense, half-disbelieving; whispers in Carnet's ear, gathers stick and hat, follows Danton's progress out.

Vestibule. *The crowd carries Danton out into the night. Handshakes, shouts. Minders jostle him through to his waiting coach. He looks around the space. Catches sight of Paine coming after him, Carnet at his side.*

PAINE: Mr Danton, Thomas Paine, I wonder if I might have your *Times*, sir ...

DANTON: Thomas **Paine**, did ye say? Old Common Sense? My God, why was I not told? My *Times*, sir, is yours. As is my heart ...

He takes Paine in his arms, kisses him beefily. The name sears through the crowd: applause, cheering, cries of Vive Monsieur Paine, Vive l'Amérique.

PAINE: *The Times* 'll do fine for the present, mister ...

DANTON: On behalf of the Club Cordeliers, on behalf of all France, Georges Jacques Danton welcomes ye, Mr Paine. Tomorrow, sir, I am yours. Tonight ... *(He smiles, catching sight of Carnet by Paine's side)* C'est toi, comme j'ai cru ... Bring Mr Paine to my house whenever he wishes and we'll talk. Take good care of this man. C'est un trésor.

(He waves, begins climbing into his carriage, greets the pair of waiting young beauties there, slaps the wig back, sticks his great mug out of the window) This man Burke should be here like you, Paine, seeing the truth of things, or his lies will harm us all ... *(To coachman)* Aux Jacobins, allez ...

U.S. Ministry coach. Night. Carriage on the move through winter trees. Inside, they sit detached in their separate processes: Carnet, wrapped in her cloak, has removed her wig and ribbon, now releases her pinned hair; Paine broods over Danton's Times.

CARNET: *(Quiet; remote)* How long will you stay with us, Paine?

He looks across at her. Pale hair floats to her shoulders, pin by pin.

PAINE: Can't say. I do have matters t'attend in England. ...

She looks up at him, pin in mouth; a dark glisten of eyes in the darkness.

CARNET: You have ... family there?

PAINE: No. *(Silence)* Folks died last year.*(He returns his eyes to the safety of the streets)* I've had a bridge made. Hope to show it in London in the Spring.

CARNET: This man who speaks against us, Burke, you know him?

PAINE: Aye. A lifelong champion of Liberty in the British parliament and until this moment a man I was happy to call friend.

CARNET: So. Perhaps ye can set him right ...

PAINE: Mm. Mebbe.

*The coach slows, Carnet looks out of the window, calls something in French to the driver. Paine stares out at the street; the **Bouche de Fer** printshop slides into view, the coach stops.*

CARNET: Eh voilà. Here, I made a list, people, places ...
You must let me know what you want of me.

PAINE: *(Studying list)* I will. Thank ye ...

Silence. He looks at her for a moment; face to face. She draws up her hood; moves by him to climb down onto the cobbles. He leans back to let her by, suddenly aware of her closeness and his need. She turns to stare at him through the window.

CARNET: Will ye go to meet with Danton tomorrow?

He gazes at her, for a moment lost again in her dark eyes.

PAINE: Mebbe. Got some thinking to do ...

CARNET: Let me know. I'll bring ye.

PAINE: Aye.

She turns away.

CARNET: *(Over her shoulder; premonitory)* Don't desert us, Paine.

He frowns, wonders if he's heard her aright, goes to answer, she's already disappearing up the stairway beside the darkened printshop. His eyes move up to the first floor; a light burns in the window. He leans back in the silence, awash with unfamiliar feeling: need, anger, unease.

PAINE: *(Mutter)* What d'ye tek me for, woman, one o' yer summer soldiers ...?

He bangs the roof with his stick, the coach rolls forward. Something glints on the floor near his feet, he stoops to gather it. It's the black ribbon from her wig. He leans back again, eyes closed, ribbon to face, scenting her there in the coach.

Tuileries. The Library. *Night. Paine pads in through the opened double doors, a liveried footman closes them behind him. He heads for his jumbled mound of belongings around the writing-desk; lays Carnet's ribbon across his pages; spreads Danton's Times for another look. Shivers. Crosses to the fireplace, steps into the hearth to stir the logs with his boot. Sudden flushing sounds of reluctant water-closet from behind the wall; an odd stumping sound, wood on wood, a panelled connecting-door cracks open, Gouverneur Morris peglegs in, fastening his breech-flap and cursing the cold. Mumbles his way to the fire. Sees Paine. Starts. Stops. Squints.*

GOUVERNEUR MORRIS: I'll be damned. Paine, is it?

PAINE: Aye. I stay here. S'my room.

GOUVERNEUR MORRIS: The Marquis had me brought here. Some ceremony, he said ...

PAINE: Be my guest.

Morris joins Paine at the fire. The two men stand in silence, warming their arses.

GOUVERNEUR MORRIS: And how are ye, Paine?

PAINE: Well, Morris. Y'self?

GOUVERNEUR MORRIS: Coping, sir. I don't grumble. What brings ye to these parts? Heard ye were building a bridge or somesuch ...

Lafayette sweeps in, a servant on his tail.

LAFAYETTE: Mr Paine, you are returned, excellent. Mr Morris has graced us with this unexpected visit, perfect for the small ceremony I am at last possible to perform ... Excuse me, gentlemen ...

He whispers instructions to the servant, marches off towards a bureau down the huge room. Remains a distant presence through what follows. Morris looks at Paine for answer.

PAINE: Aye, I'm building a bridge. Lookin' for buyers.

GOUVERNEUR MORRIS: Really. In revolutionary France? The only thing they're buying here just now is hot air and stuff 'n' nonsense. The cockade of success has gone to their heads, there's agitators at every street corner sowing dissension, inventing "rights" for all and sundry, gnawing away at the natural order of things. Let's hope our friend Lafayette there can keep 'em down or there'll be blood in the gutters here till the Last Trump ... They're sharing power with their **king**, for God's sake! Isn't that enough? The "Revolution" is over. The French need to get back to making money, then maybe somebody'll buy your bridge ... (*Chuckles; crosses to the desk; sees The Times. The servant returns, crusted claret and flagons on a tray in his hands*) I see you're keeping abreast, Mr Paine. Mr Burke's outburst in the English Parliament has caused quite a rumpus, I can tell ye.

PAINE: I bet.

He turns deliberately, spits into the fire. Morris rubs his hands, enjoying Paine's growing discomfort.

MORRIS: Friend o' yours, am I right? (*Paine says nothing*) Did he tell ye he's been preparing a book on the subject? Word is he has it all but ready for the printer's ... (*Paine squints a look at him, keying in.*) Thank God, say I. That should put paid to the nonsense-mongers once and for all, nobody better in the English language or higher in public esteem ...

The servant fills their flagons, withdraws. Lafayette approaches, a fine silver casket in his hands.

LAFAYETTE: Gentlemen, it has long been my wish to present my dear friend President Washington with a token of this nation's esteem, and through an envoy who has earned the undying gratitude of America for the part he had in the creation of her freedoms. Both token and envoy are at last to hand. *(He lifts the casket lid. A large metal key stares up from the red satin)* The key to the Bastille prison. The symbol of our liberty. *(Morris begins to wipe his palm on his britches, clear in his mind he's the one)* Carry it safely , Mr Paine, for it is charged with history ...

Paine takes the box, stares at the key, thanks him quietly. Lafayette hands them flagons, raises his.

LAFAYETTE: The Revolution!

Morris's face; Paine's. The wine glasses. The wine sways bloodily on the touch.

Mix slowly to

Paine's pen dipping for ink; hovering over a piece of Lafayette's embossed notepaper; beginning to write: Dear Mr Short,

PAINE'S VOICE: Forgive the abruptness of my departure. I have left a letter for Mr Jefferson on the desk, which you will kindly forward to him by the next pouch ...

ENGLAND, 1791, Summer. Large country house at Beaconsfield, snug in its six hundred acres. Paine's carriage clops up the long treelined avenue to the house.

PAINE'S LETTER VOICE CONTINUED: Please be good enough to assure my young instructress that my business in England is largely France's ...

Close shot of Paine staring out at the house ahead.

PAINE'S VOICE: ... lest she take my absence for desertion ...

Wentworth House. *Drawing Room, ill-kempt, sunk beneath the ages, dark and chill. Paine stands by a window, reading the dank space amid the click of many clocks and the alphabetic mutterings of a Caribbean parrot with a Dublin brogue.*

A man enters abruptly, stands for a moment as if lost; he's midsixties, oddeyed, a shambles.

MAN: *(The parrot's Dublin voice)* Mr Paine, sir.

PAINE: Mr Burke.

BURKE: I cannot see ye, sir. I'm at my desk.

PAINE: Be happy to wait. But my business is urgent.

Silence. Burke loses track for a moment, begins to mumble a line he's been struggling with.

BURKE: Sit.

Paine takes the proffered chair, Burke slumps into his, face cowled in gloom.

PAINE: I'm conscious of intrusion, Mr Burke, and will be brief ...

BURKE: ... If it is France ye would discuss, I have told ye all I wish to upon the subject ...

PAINE: Ye've told me nothing, sir. My letters lie unanswered.

BURKE: Precisely, sir. On events in that miserable place, I am not persuadable.

PAINE: Not even by the truth ...?

BURKE: I believe I know the truth, Mr Paine. At the moment I am busy wrestling it down onto paper.

A clock strikes the quarter; another follows; another. Burke takes out a pocket watch; stares at the silver face-cover for some moments, puts it away. Paine watches.

PAINE: Mr Burke, ye did much for the rights of colonial Americans, ye've spent a lifetime championing the cause of slaves and religious dissenters, ye opposed the pillorying of the sodomites. Men and women have read your works and learnt the future need not be, must not be, as appalling and oppressive as the past. Yet now, when **millions** pay you heed by tearing up the

125

fraudulent contract with history that holds them down and demanding their natural human rights, ye turn on 'em like any mad monarch and vilify them. Why? In reason's name, sir, why?

BURKE: *(standing abruptly)* Mr Paine, ye may find your answer on the shelves at seven shillings and sixpence when my book is published. I have nothing more to say to you.

Paine rises slowly. Frowns a little.

PAINE: Ye'll not come to France with me and see for yerself?

BURKE: I will not, sir.

PAINE: Then I'll be plain. Publish your book and I will answer it.

Silence. Horses neigh nearby; Paine checks a window: a bulldog stands on hindlegs at the pane, staring jowlily in.

BURKE: Ye're a living danger to all that's sacred in human affairs, Mister Paine. "The French Revolution is but the forerunner to others across Europe ...", one of your letters said. You agitate your way across the world, sowing dissension, breeding conflict, gnawing away at the settled natural order of things. And here you are back in your own land and about to put it to the torch. *(Paine watches him in rapt fascination, the man's madness suddenly vivid before his eyes)* But ye will not succeed, sir. Thanks to our sullen resistance to innovation, thanks to the cold sluggishness of our national character, we British still bear the stamp of our forefathers. Use what art ye may, ye'll not root out of this people's mind the principles of natural subordination. They will continue to respect that property of which they cannot partake, they will continue to labour to obtain what by labour can be obtained; and when they find, as they commonly do, the success disproportionate to the endeavour, they will continue to be taught to seek their consolation in the final proportions of eternal justice ...

PAINE: *(Eventually; deadly quiet)* While you, sir, the Champion of Liberty, will continue to call yourself a Whig and receive a secret pension of ten thousand a year from the Tories to trash the future.

BURKE: Leave my house, sir. I had imagined you a gentleman.

PAINE: No, sir. I'm an American. Proud of it.

He heads for the door; the parrot scolds the dank air: "A, B, C ..."

PAINE'S WRITING VOICE: Not one glance of compassion, not one commiserating reflection has Mr Burke bestowed on those who linger out the most wretched of lives, a life without hope ...

LONDON. Autumn. Tiny cottage room, Marylebone. Paine in a fume of writing, hair long again, tousled; a scrubby salt-and-pepper beard; trousers, bare feet. His landlady (Mary Rickman) works around him, laying out his working supper where she can: cold meat, cheese, bread, milk. Clio Rickman, bookseller, old friend, pops his head round the door, smiles fondly at Paine's antics. Desk and room are alive with manuscript. There's rum next to the ink; a book by Paine's hand, frequently consulted: Burke's "Reflections on the French Revolution."

PAINE'S VOICE: It is painful to behold a man employing his talents to corrupt himself. Nature has been kinder to Mr Burke than he has been to her. He is not affected by the reality of distress touching his heart, but by the showy resemblance of it striking his imagination ...

London Street. Night. Winter. Paine and long-time friend Clio Rickman sit in a carriage while a London publisher (Johnson) sits opposite reading Paine's MS by lamplight. Echoes of Bell, Race Street and the publication of "Common Sense".

PAINE'S VOICE: ... As it is not difficult to perceive that hereditary governments are verging to their decline, and that Revolutions on the broad basis of national sovereignty and government by representation are making their way in Europe, it would be an act of wisdom to anticipate their approach, and produce Revolutions by reason and accommodation, rather than commit them to the issue of convulsions. For this **is** an Age of Revolutions ...

The publisher closes the MS, finished; looks across at Paine, nods, moved; offers Paine his hand on the deal.

PAINE'S VOICE: ... in which everything may be looked for.

Rickman's cottage garden. *Late winter day. Paine stands in his greatcoat in the vegetable plot, cracking blackened bean-pods into his hand and fingering them into a linen draw-bag. Rickman knocks at the kitchen window, face glum, signals him in.*

Kitchen. Paine hugs Mary Rickman goodbye, gathers his travel gear, heads out into the front bookshop, sees the coach outside and two men watching the cottage from the other side of the road. Lays down his bags to look for Rickman. Crosses to the doorway of the cubbyhole office. Sees Rickman in sombre talk with two men.

PAINE: I'm away, Clio, coach is arrived ...

RICKMAN: Hold the horses, Tom, ye've company ... This here's John Frost and young Tom Christie from the Revolution Society, that's their coach, they're come hotfoot from your Publisher's ...

PAINE: Ye got my book proofs, Mr Frost?

FROST: Johnson's pulled out, lawyer's opinion he could go to prison, lose his business, government's had spies on the shop since he took the work ...

PAINE: Damn 'em, the Mad King have bought ten thousand of the Burke book and sent it to every notable in the land, I can't even find a publisher not in terror of his life ...

CHRISTIE: It's done, sir. I've found a man. *(Paine blinks at the brighteyed young man)* He's less to lose and eager to proceed.

PAINE: 'S his name?

CHRISTIE: Doesn't want it known until he's issued. But he's a good man, ye have my word.

Paine looks hard at Christie, notes the revolutionary cockade in his hat; then to Rickman for help.

RICKMAN: Young Christie's Dr Priestley's nephew. Decent pedigree, I'd say.

PAINE: Mm. Mr Christie, I'm obliged. Ye'll send me copies on, will ye?

CHRISTIE: *(A nod)* There's a pair here ye might like to take with ye, Johnson had 'em sewn up for ye from galley, his way o' saying sorry ... *(Paine takes the package. A second coach slides to a halt outside the window)* ... for the setback.

PAINE: Setback? Best news I've had all year. Ye think we're gonna get where we're headed by grace and favour? I tell ye, when each one of us has an agent on his tail - like the pair outside the window there - when they start passing emergency laws to put us all away, packing special juries and sending paid mobs to howl outside our homes, we'll know we're getting somewhere ...

He leaves for the shop, his bags, the coach. Rickman follows him.

RICKMAN: Any idea when ye'll be back? *(Paine shakes his head)* What about yer bridge?

PAINE: There's time for bridges.

They shake hands; friends from way back.

Boat at sea. *Deck. Close shot of Paine's hand, a book in it, resting on ship's rail.*

PAINE'S WRITING VOICE: To George Washington, That the rights of man may become as universal as your benevolence can wish, and that you may enjoy the happiness of seeing the New World regenerate the Old, is the prayer of Thomas Paine ...

*The shot clarifies on the title: **Rights of Man: Part First.**

PARIS, 1791 Paine's coach crawls along the approach roads to the Tuileries. Sounds of a clamorous demonstration grow steadily louder. People run past the coach window to swell the crowd up ahead. Cries, slogans, songs, placards: the King must sign or the King must go ... Paine's face at the window, a touch worried by the violence of the rage felt and shown outside. The coach passes the gates to the King's Residence: several squads of armed National Guards stand interposed between gates and crowd in a fragile stand-off.

DRIVER: Presque là, Monsieur ...

PAINE: Bon. Merci.

Lafayette's library and balcony. View from balcony of the great square linking Lafayette's palace with that of the King. An élite squad of National Guards is being stood down, another takes its place, protectors of the King's safety. Sounds of protest in the distance. Paine, on balcony, reading the scene. Louis XVI, in his day clothes, stands watching the ceremony from his huge terrace. Lafayette, on great white horse, sword drawn, gives the King a ceremonial salute. Louis raises his hat in response.

SHORT: *(From behind him)* Mr Paine, welcome back, sir ...

Paine turns, sees Short being shown down the long room by a footman. Waves him over to the desk area, already recolonised by Paine's gear and papers; joins him.

PAINE: *(Handshake)* Good to see ye, Willie, sorry it took so long ...

SHORT: *(Laying fat file of cuttings on desk)* Been following your progress in the English presses, ye've bin busy alright, guess Mr Burke's put in his place ... *(Paine spreads the cuttings, glances over them)* Ye heard from Mr Jefferson ...? *(Paine nods)* No word on who'll replace him. But it's bad ...

PAINE: Tell me what's happenin' out there, Willie, feels like things're comin' off the hooks ...

SHORT: It ain't good, Mr Paine. In brief: the Assembly's come up with a new Constitution, brought ye the Ministry copy, I'll need it back ... *(Lays it on desk)* Lot o' pressure on 'em from below, Louis won't sign it, says it's unholy and ungodly, the Clubs and Sections are putting people on the streets under the slogan Sign or Resign, Lafayette's turning his troops on the demonstrators and begins to look as if he's taking the King's side ... There's more, but ye have the bones ...

Paine sniffs, dips a pen, writes something in a copy of "Rights of Man".

PAINE: An' who's stirrin' the people, Willie?

SHORT: The Jacobins're doin' plenty, Marat and his paper *The Friend of the People*, Danton down at the Cordeliers, there's no lack o' leaders ...

PAINE: See Danton gets this, will ye. Ask if he'll see me. *(Inscribes the second copy)* And have this carried round to Miss Carnet, if ye will. Like her to do the French translation, guess I'm gonna need her help again gettin' around. Got to find a way to be useful ...

SHORT: *(Preparing to leave)* Mind if I read it, sir? I could do it tonight ...

PAINE: Help yerself. *(Silence. Soft)* Must've offered Mr Jefferson somethin' big, to get him out o' France.

SHORT: Secretary of State.

PAINE: *(Whistles)* Well, if it helps him to the Presidency next time, it won't all be bad ...

SHORT: There's a room booked at White's on the Ministry's account, if ye'd rather.

PAINE: This'll do. Find yer way out?

Short smiles, glad he's back. Leaves. Paine flicks a page or two of the copy constitution, from the square below a sentry calls and is answered, the voices echoic, unreal; he wanders back to the balcony, stares out at the square.

131

Lamps have been lit against the dark. In the gloom, he watches the lone figure of Lafayette posting his guards in fours around the vast space. The horse gleams, ghostly.

Narrow street, St Antoine district. *The approaches to Danton's political offices in the final house of a tall terrace, where a crowd of a hundred or so of Paris's poorest listen to an address from the first-floor balcony. The driver calls: Eh voilà citoyen; the US Ministry coach slows to a halt. Paine walks the remaining yards, joins the crowd at its fringe; takes in the balcony - Hanriot, Danton and, in full ecstatic flood, the strange swarthy dwarflike figure of the Friend of the People, Marat.*

MARAT: *(in French)* ... I ask again, dear friends, who will rule France? That dull bloodsucking traitor Louis who has the audacity to call himself King? (*The crowd: No!*) The aristocrat party holding sway in our Assembly under the Marquis on a White Horse? (*No!*) It is the **People** who will be sovereign ... (*Aye, the People!*) the shock-troops of Liberty to whom all France now turns for its future peace and happiness ... (*The people, the people!*) My word on it, dear friends, if blood has to be shed for the future of France and all humanity, let the blood of Jean-Paul Marat, the Friend of the People, be the first to flow ...

He draws a primed pistol from his belt, holds it operatically to his head. The crowd screams NO, NO, NO ... A shout rings out from a lookout on the roof; sounds of horses hooves on cobblestones, the crowd swings round to face the threat; Danton pushes a wholly unresisting Marat back into the house; whispers instructions to Hanriot, who disappears inside; calls Calmez-vous, mes amis to the folk below.

A dozen mounted National Guard thread their way through the crowd into the tiny square below the balcony. A young lieutenant holds up a scrolled document.

LIEUTENANT: *(To Balcony)* I have a warrant here, signed by the elected Mayor of Paris, for the arrest of Monsieur Marat. Who speaks for this gathering?

DANTON: Georges Jacques Danton, elected President of the District of St Antoine. *(Cheers)* Send yer warrant up, sir.

He nods to a claqueur below; the Lieutenant hands it over, already wrong-footed, the claqueur hurries it upstairs.

LIEUTENANT: I believe it would be sensible to disperse this mob, sir

DANTON: I see no mob, sir. I see a peaceful gathering of citizens. *(The warrant arrives. He takes it.)* Right, let's see. *(Scans it)* Mm. *(Shakes his head)* Worthless. Take the word of a lawyer. *(He throws the scroll down to the cobbles. The lieutenant gives an order, draws his sword, his men go to follow)* Put it up, sir. Stay calm and look around ye.

(Hanriot silently leads clusters of men to the edges of the crowd, primitively armed with clubs, scythes and the odd rusting pike: the District's shock-troops. The horsed soldiers tic about the shrivelling space, all exits suddenly barred.) Soldiers, listen to me. *(He dons his vivid Presidential Sash of Office)* As President of this District, charged by those I serve to defend the Revolution, I urge you conduct yourselves peacably, trust me, a warrant must be supported by a court summons itemising the charges, where is it? Ye don't have one. So: return to your Town Hall across the river, and have yer masters get ye one, and serve yer warrant properly if ye still think it's worth the candle. But I promise ye, ye'll need a few more than twelve, there's a strong belief in a man's right to free speech in these parts, we didn't bring the National Guard of Paris into being so that you could shut our mouths up ... *(Shots of the Guards, listening, a tad drawn; the lieutenant, just too small for the job)* Make way, friends, let these patriots through, brothers among brothers, someone hand the young man the warrant there ...

The lieutenant decides; begins to pick a delicate way through the parting crowd; his men follow, grateful; applause slowly builds from the crowd. Paine joins it. Danton sees him, smiles, waves him in.

Small drawing room *in District Office building. An old man wheezes around the room, turning up lamps against the gloom. The lamps in turn light up Action maps of Paris, some of France, one of the world, filling the walls. Danton's dipping his head and hair in a bowl of water on the table, stripped to the waist. Paine picks at a tray of food by his armchair: bread, cheese, chunks of chicken. The debris of an earlier platter lies at his feet. They've talked long.*

DANTON: *(Strong idiomatic English)* ... This too is the Revolution, Paine, sitting, supping, talking first principles, a pair of almost strangers getting on like almost friends. *(Grins)* Ye're a good man, mister. Ye'll forgive me, I speak at the Jacobin this evening, I s'll need time to prepare ...

PAINE: (Mouth full; swigging wine) Will I go?

DANTON: There's time. In any case, we're not finished. *(A runner comes in with a scrawled note, Danton scans it, nods, the man leaves. Danton towels himself)* On ends, agreement between us ain't hard to find, mm? A sovereign people, a republic bedded in the rule of law, under a freely arrived at constitution, some form of representative government, not a hair between us. On means, *(Selects with care the gear he'll wear for his Jacobin Club address. Begins to dress before a glass, as if donning costume)* I tell ye plain, friend, while I share yer repugnance for civil violence and excess, I know one simple fact you appear to be unconscious of ... *(Smoothes his jacket on; turns to preparing his beard, chunky slashes with a knife to make it seem barbarous)* Violence and excess have stalked this land for centuries, lash, axe and dungeon have always been a King's answer to the people's cry for justice, and as we have learnt so shall we do ... Yes, there are dangers in unlocking pent-up hatreds and nursed resentments, but what choice do we have, my friend, ye think the toffs running France right now give a monkey's tosser for the rights of the poor ...? They're too busy carving up the spoils we've put into their lap ... *(He's ready, the transformation complete: dips a finger into an inkwell, haunts below his eyes with actorly dabs the Jacobin's idea of the Wild Man.)* How do I look? Wild enough ...? The Jacobins love charisma ... *(Paine shrugs; not interested)* That's another thing ye don't understand, Paine. We're **all** actors: Mirabeau, Lafayette, Louis, Marat, me ... We find or invent our roles day by day, on the stage we call the Revolution. To play well, my friend, means ye must call on more than just this, as you suppose ... *(He taps his head)* ye must call on this ... *(His heart)* and on this ... *(His cock)* Everything ye know, everything ye feel, everything you are ... I fear for ye here, Mister Paine, lest your innocence lead ye into the mire ...

PAINE: *(Readying for off)* Don't worry about me, friend. I've made my point and I'll make my way. Some things I do know. Iron rusts. Lies rot the soul. Violence and excess are a whirlpool that carry all to hell. That's all I say. My heart is with ye ...

The runner returns, whispers in Danton's ear, he nods.

DANTON: Your Mr Short's come for ye, he waits in the coach, old Runnerbean there'll tek ye out the back, the front's watched ... Take good care, eh? Write more books, that's where yer greatness lies ... The stage is yours.

Paine salutes him from the doorway, the runner leads him down a passageway, through a hole punched into next door's wall and down the stairs to a back yard. Short waves to him from the Ministry carriage in the alleyway beyond.

In the carriage, Paine reads a letter, a printed card attached to it. Outside in the streets, echoic shouts of desperate people on the move. Short watches Paine, who returns letter and card to envelope, rests his head back, eyes closed.

SHORT: Bad news is it, sir?

PAINE: No no. Seems my book's doin' its work back in England. Revolution Society invites me to speak at some Grand Bastille Day celebration in London ... England in turmoil. Takes my breath ...

SHORT: An' will ye go?

Paine gives no answer, eyes on the street.

PAINE: Where are we?

SHORT: Almost there.

PAINE: *(To driver)* Hold up on the corner, will ye? *(To Short)* Got a call to make, give me a minute ...

*He gets out at the corner, heads for the **Bouche de Fer** printshop, pushes through the helpers on the pavement waiting for fly-bills to take onto the streets. Short watches anxiously as Paine disappears inside the shop.*

Inside the printshop a woman carrying a child leads him down the congested din of the shop towards a young man, spectacled, earnest, busy supervising the work. The man bends close to catch his name, smiles at once when he hears it, embraces him in greeting, beckons him to follow to a rear stair-passage to the commune upstairs.

YOUNG MAN: *(Leading him in)* De Bonneville, sir. A pleasure. Come.

Paine frowns, follows him in. The place is almost bare of furnishings: table, a few chairs, paillasses on the wood floors. An open staircase leads to an upper floor. A young woman sits sleeping on a bed by the far window, her back to the wall, an infant at each tit, asleep too. De Bonneville looks for something, finds it, brings it back to the table.

DE BONNEVILLE: Yes, she certainly received it, see ... *(Paine studies the Ministry wrapping, the black ribbon he used to tie it in)* I can't say if she's translating it, she is her own law ...

PAINE: She's not here ...?

DE BONNEVILLE: Holland. She sets up a new journal.

PAINE: Ah. When's she expected ...?

DE BONNEVILLE: Whenever. *(Paine nods, dealing with disappointment)* May I help?

PAINE: No no. *(Picks up a fly-bill from the table)* Ye seem to have plenty enough on yer plate ...

DE BONNEVILLE: *(Moving down room)* We say the King must go ... *(One of the infants has begun to cry, he gently uncouples it from the sleeping woman's tit, carries it back on his shoulder)* How can a King lead a revolution?

PAINE: Good question.

DE BONNEVILLE: Maybe ye will ask it in our Assembly, the Philosopher of Revolution has much weight there. *(The baby yowls, chews the air)* This one has weight too, eh? Benjamin. Like his mother, no? *(Paine glances at the sleeping woman down the room, doesn't see it, nods anyway)* I tell Carnet ye came. She'll be happy, she speak of you much ...

Paine tickles the kid's cheek with a finger; smiles at the father.

PAINE: Thank ye.

Lafayette's library. *Night. The vast room, Paine enisled in desklight, working hard, pen to paper. The desk, several letters, mounds of notes. Over this,*

PAINE'S WRITING VOICE: *(fragments)* ... Notes: Rights of Man Part Second ... The dangers to which the success of revolutions is most exposed ... is that of attempting them before the principles on which they proceed, and the advantages to result from them, are sufficiently seen and ... Dear Mr Jefferson, I spent a couple of intriguing hours with Monsieur Danton recently and wonder if ye have an opinion to share with me on the man. I must say he left me in some gloom about where we are headed here, though I liked him much ... Dear Carney, I inquired at your lodgings to ask if ye'd received my book and learnt ye were in ...

A sound from the square outside brings him to for a moment: The Guard being stood down. He frowns, checks his watch: past midnight. He picks up the Carnet letter, looks at it, nose wrinkling; wanders to the balcony with it in his hand. Arrives in time to see the stood-down Guard being marched away through the main gates. Searches for the new Guard to be posted, finds none. Looks at the letter.

PAINE'S VOICE: ... I plan to lodge at White's for the remainder of my stay. Should ye return before the early days of July, when I may have to spend a brief time in London, perhaps ye could ...

He looks up. Lamps have appeared on the King's terrace. A huge black six-horse berlin carriage draws up at the steps, the lamps light several cloaked figures down the steps to enter it. Their low voices carry across the still space for a moment, the berlin draws away, fades beneath an archway.

Paine sniffs. Looks briefly at the letter, scrunches it. Goes back inside.

Lafayette's library, pre-dawn. *Still dark. A clock in the room gathers to strike five. Paine lies sleepless on his iron cot. He stares balefully across at the clock; listens to its hissing wind-up to the strike.*

The door crashes open, Lafayette stumbles in, crosses to collect his ceremonial sword from the mantel wall, calls Paine to wake in a shrill, fearful voice. Servants pour after him in night gear, summoned from sleep. Lafayette's half-dressed, general's jacket unbuttoned, britches unflapped, nightcap flopping on his head.

LAFAYETTE: *(French invading now-precarious English; under stress)* ... The birds have flew the cup, Paine. I am undone, sir, all is lost, the shame, the shame ...

PAINE: ... I'm not sure I have your meaning, sir ...

LAFAYETTE: *(After torrent of French; struggling with his sword)* ... The King and Queen are gone, sir, fled in the night I know not where, he will not sign the constitution, I will be blamed, I am his keeper, charged by the Assembly t'keep him secured, they'll say I plotted his escape. There'll be a rising, there'll be a **revolution** ...

PAINE: Ye **have** a revolution, General. An' it don't need a king. Let him go, sir. Whatever ye do, don't let the bugger back ...

LAFAYETTE: *(A servant buttoning his breeches)* I am undone. I am lost. I fall from grace ...

He dismisses the servants in a flurry of instructions. Sinks slowly to one knee, his hands covering his weeping face. Paine watches a moment, slowly moved by the man's pain; gets to his feet, pads over. Lafayette weeps on, as if alone. Paine reaches out a hesitant hand to his shoulder.

PAINE: Come, friend. We'll survive.

Lafayette looks up, eyes bloodshot, hopeless.

White's Hotel. *Paine's room. He stands at a window, bags by him, his greatcoat laid across them, cockaded hat atop all, watching the streets below. In his point of view, the hot, sticky pavements, jammed solid with citizens waiting in sombre silence for scheduled arrivals; scans left, right: a sense of the whole of Paris stuffed with the same.*

SHORT: *(Arriving)* Sorry I'm late, sir. Bloody crowd ...

PAINE: Damned fools have gone and caught him, am I right? *(Short nods)* It'll cost 'em.

SHORT: They bring him back to troop him through the city ...

PAINE: Bad news. Will I make the boat?

SHORT: Ye're still intent on leaving, are ye, sir?

PAINE: S'a coupla weeks. Ye get the visa? *(Short hands him a Ministry envelope)* Anything else?

SHORT: A letter from Mr Jefferson, sir ... *(Hands it him)*

PAINE: Good. Any word who comes in his stead ...?

SHORT: Only rumour, sir. All bad ... And *(Sifting through his bundle of mails)* ... Had it here somewhere ...

PAINE: Calais coach leaves at four, is it?

SHORT: *(Still searching)* Four it is, sir. Got it. *(Hands Paine a book tied in black ribbon, a note tucked in it.)* Miss Carnet, sir. Dropped by with it yesterday evening, just back from Amsterdam, I believe ... *(Street din builds, shouts, the splatter of horses' hooves on cobblestone)* If ye'll excuse me a moment, I may have left something below ...

Short heads off. Paine holds book and note for some while, alarmed perhaps at the feelings they arouse. Fiddles finally for his specs. Opens the note. Reads the brief message. Checks the book. Checks his watch. Returns to the note. A huge roar from the street; closer. He gathers his stick, heads for the still open door.

Short's back, a bill in his hand.

SHORT: Yer bill, sir. In my damned pocket all the time. Thirteen bottles of rum, is that ... (right)?

PAINE: A man takes that many, ye think he's counting? Watch the bags, Willie. Back in a tick ...

Heads off. Short frowns, begins to follow.

SHORT: Mr. Paine ...?

PAINE: ... Stretch my legs.

Short's stranded in the doorway, charged with the bags; watches Paine disappear down the stairs to the Lobby.

SHORT: Mr Paine, sir, stay indoors, it's but an hour to the coach, ye could be in danger out there ... *(Thinks of something, swivels back into the room, sees the discarded cockaded hat, rushes it across to the open window. Calling down)* At least wear your goddamned hat, sir, ye'll be taken for a King's man! Mr Paine!

Paris Streets. *Paine pushes purposefully through the moil, all Paris out to see the Royals returned. The silence is deathly, unnerving. Several people address him curtly in French, twirl a finger round their cockades to ask where his is. Paine presses on, into rougher territory. Is finally stopped by a sudden forward surge of people at the rattle of coach wheels approaching. Sees, above massed silent heads, the jog-jog of Lafayette's stiff mounted frame, sword drawn, at the head of the sombre procession. A huge black berlin slides by on his tail, six black cockaded horses, royal faces glimpsed inside the shadowed coach; a second Berlin, a child's face staring blankly out. And gone.*

*Paine scans the silent, unbudging crowd for a way through. Finds himself staring at a hoisted kid staring at him. Tries to push on. The kid yells something, points at him. Shouts build around him, hands grab him, mouths snarl questions, feet trip him, he's down. Boots, fists, spittle rain down on him. A cry goes up: **À la lanterne!** A noosed rope appears, hands slide it over his head. He's dragged bloodily to his feet. Falls immediately back to the ground.*

*New voices intervene. Glimpse of a familiar face through the ruck: De Bonneville, fiercely spelling out the crowd's misplaced hostility. One of his assailants reaches in to shake Paine's hand, others help him to his feet. De Bonneville wipes blood from his face with a copy of **Bouche de Fer.***

DE BONNEVILLE: *(Struggling with his spectacles)* Ye can ... promenade? *(Paine nods, in shock still).* Come. We're nearto.

The Commune kitchen. *Paine's stripped to the waist, being cleaned and iodined by De Bonneville. He has a fair bit of bruising, face cuts, a nicked ear, a heavy slicing rip across his right side, kidney level. A woman sings a lullaby in the room above.*

DE BONNEVILLE: *(Surveying him)* I think you live, Paine. Here. *(Hands him cockaded hat)* You wear this to home. No hat, no head today. *(Calling)* Eh, tu es là?

WOMAN'S VOICE: *(Barely heard)* Sh. Il dort.

DE BONNEVILLE: *(To Paine)* You rest a minute, eh?

He tiptoes away. Paine stands gingerly, already stiffening. The hat's too small for his large head. Checks his watch.

CARNET: *(Arrived on open staircase)* Paine?

He turns. Sees her. She holds the sleeping Benjamin in her arms, her bodice undone, the right breast still exposed from the feed. She moves into the room, searches for something on a dresser. He watches her, his bruised brain slowly putting child and woman together.

CARNET: Wait. Let me lay this one down.

He stands in shadow, watching her.

CARNET: *(Arriving, seeing him)* Mon dieu. Are you all right?

PAINE: The crowd took me for a king-lover. I'll live.

CARNET: Sit down, let me look ...

PAINE: I have to go. I have a coach ...

CARNET: Sit.

He takes a chair. She sits close to look him over.

CARNET; Who tended you?

PAINE: De Bonneville. He also saved my life.

CARNET: *(Beginning to look for it)* This needs potash ...

PAINE: No, no. It's not ... *(She searches on)* I was on my way to say ... *(Shows her the book)* Thank ye for this.

CARNET: It made me happy, to read, to work on, to have your trust ... *(By the cot)* Do you like my boy? He's named after Franklin ...

PAINE: *(Hobbling to look)* He's a beauty. Like his mother.

She flicks a look at him. Holds a moment. Looks away.

142

CARNET: No, no. He's like de Bonneville. Look at the nose.

Silence. Paine tries to assemble it.

PAINE: De Bonneville's your husband?

CARNET: No. De Bonneville's the father. Sometimes, when we desire it, we'll lie together, this time I miscounted my days. Et voilà. This perfect creature. *(Silence. She looks up at him)* We make new worlds, Paine. Invent the future. We cannot do it shackled to the past. Did you not write it yourself? "We are upon experiments," yes?

PAINE: Well, as I remember it, we were makin' up a new constitution for Pennsylvania at the time ...

She laughs, free, open. He lifts himself up with care.

CARNET: Will I be honest with you, Paine?

PAINE: I guess ye will, Carney.

CARNET: *(Quite serious)* There was a time, last year, I experienced a strong desire to lie with **you**. *(He shakes his head a little, unsettled, deeply adrift)* Perhaps ye knew it. If ye're honest.

He sniffs. Shakes his head again.

PAINE: Hoped mebbe. Feared. Considered the. Impossibilities. Knew it? *(Shakes his head)* Carney, I know less and less ... *(Raises the book, a sort of goodbye)* Will I. Write ye?

CARNET: Where d'ye go?

PAINE: *(Shrugs)* I speak in London. Bastille Day celebrations.

CARNET: Our papers say you're a marked man there, will ye come back?

PAINE: I will.

CARNET: Then ye may write me.

He drifts in her gaze a moment longer. Nods. Leaves. She stands, crosses into the living room, waits to watch him reach the street and head off.

Over this:

PAINE'S VOICE: *(outdoor public meeting)* ...Were twenty shillings given immediately on the birth of a child, to every woman who should make the demand, a great deal of instant distress would be relieved ... And twenty shillings to every newmarried couple as of right, to put them on the way ...

ENGLAND, 1792, **London.** Bowling green, rear of Angel Inn. Faces in the crowd, men, women, kids, listening to their Tom Paine speak. Paine gives his address from a tall box-rostrum erected at the back wall of the inn, shared with Committee members and celebrities of the radical movement, Rickman, Christie, Frost among them. Banners shout the occasion: **Bastille Day Celebration; London Revolution Society; Thomas Paine.**

PAINE: *(Manuscript in hand for reference)* ... And to every poor family, four pounds a year for every child under 14 years of age; and for each of those children ten shillings more for the expense of schooling ... A pension as of right to all who reach the age of fifty. And all found from the taxes we pay - I've done the costing - The millions wasted on government are more than enough to reform most evils and to benefit the condition of every person in the nation ... *(He holds up his MS-in-progress: **Rights of Man Two**)* Now, friends, a word to the Government spies who might be hidden among you: tell your sorry masters, all this, and a great deal more, will appear in my new book, which I propose to publish this year in a sixpenny edition so that millions may read it, ye may stop some from speakin' their mind, ye'll not stop Tom Paine ...

*Excited applause, gasps, shrieks, shouts. Paine winks across at Christie. Sees Rickman scanning the crowd, concerned at something out there. A hissing sound. Something hits Paine on the cheeks, draws blood. Two Committee members go down, struck by something. Paine stoops to collect the missile: a metal hob nail stud with initials stamped on its head: **TP**. Christie grabs him by the arm, begins to tug him to the safety of the inn. Paine looks out at the crowd. Folk cower under a sustained barrage of metal thrown over the surrounding walls, their version of the cluster-bomb.*

Sudden ugly shouts at the perimeters; gangs of club-swinging thugs leap the wall, men in the crowd begin a defence, heads begin to get cracked.

CHRISTIE: Come, let's get ye away, it's you they're after ...

PAINE: Dammit, man, I haven't finished ...

RICKMAN: *(Taking his other arm, pushing him on. Dry.)* You're finished. Trust me.

The two thrust him indoors. Sound fades slowly.

Move to

Rural Kent. *Autumn day. A solitary rider pushes his sturdy grey workhorse across a sweep of rolling field. Turns on the crest of a hill to look back at the tiny isolated cottage below. Smoke wisps upwards from its pot chimneys. Over this:*

PAINE'S VOICE: *(as if in talk, outdoors)* ... I find myself holed away for safety's sake in a monk's cell in the back country, friends see I'm fed and watered by the week and carry what pages I've written to the printer ...

A small gulley in a copse. Early winter. Paine sits with his back to a tree, reading a half-finished letter to his tethered horse, who's drinking from a stream, uninterested.

PAINE'S VOICE: ... The authorities know I have another piece coming, agents scour the land for sight of it, if I'm taken before the book's done there won't be a publisher in Britain prepared to print ... *(He looks across at the horse. Nothing. Throws a clump of earth at it.)* Hey, I'm talking to ye, look at me ...

The horse swings his big head, shows his teeth. Paine returns the grin.

Cottage. *Night. Mounded manuscript sits on the table. Paine squats before the stone hearth, going through stuff in his cracked cowhide satchel. Finds Lotte's drawing of him; a note from Marthe; Rittenhouse's compass, the name bold on the base.*

PAINE'S VOICE: Why is it that scarcely any are executed but the poor? When, in countries that are called civilised, we see age going to the workhouse and youth to the gallows, something must be wrong in the system of government ...

*His hand draws out the French stuff; a copy of **Bouche de Fer**; Carnet's rough-print copy of **Les Droits de l'Homme**; her small note inside it.*

CARNET'S VOICE: *(as he scans it)* Do not despair, Paine. The future is ours. In true friendship. Carney.

Moonlit bedroom. *Paine on his back on the bed, staring at the cracked irregularities of the ancient ceiling. Fragments of the past year in England invade the plaster: secret fireside talks with reformers in public house backrooms; firelit hillside meetings; torchlit processions ... Over this:*

PAINE'S VOICE: ... There is a smell of good things coming, the people begin to stir, reason and revolution walk hand in hand now and the book is almost done ...

Countryside. *First days of Spring. Paine leads his horse through a copse of trees. Stoops to examine something. Close shot of the twig in his hand.*

PAINE'S VOICE: It is now towards the end of winter ... And I observe a single bud has begun to swell. Would I not reason very unnaturally to suppose **this** the only bud in England so enlarged ...?

Mounted now, he canters the grey across fat fields.

PAINE'S VOICE: ... I grant the vegetable sleep will continue on some trees longer than on others. But all will be in leaf in the summer ...

He's reined down to a walk, negotiates the track to the safe house, eyes wary, alert.

PAINE'S VOICE: ... The book is out. The hunt is on. I'm charged with criminal libel, the land teems with Lawmen out to serve the writ of summons ...

He dismounts, unsaddles, slaps the horse into its paddock, heads for the cottage door.

PAINE'S VOICE: Working men and women sing my praises, others burn my effigy in the streets, but I become invisible, day by day, even to myself ... Celebrity may turn the head, it will never quicken the blood ...

Someone calls his name close by. He freezes, scents, scans. His name again, from above. Sees a man, high in a tree, notebook on lap, gazing down on him.

PAINE: Who're you?

MAN: William Blake.

PAINE: What're ye up to?

BLAKE: Penning a poem.

PAINE: What're ye doing here?

BLAKE: If you're Thomas Paine, I'm saving yer life.

Dover Harbour. *Day. Late summer. Paine stands in a line of people, waiting to board ship. Up ahead, two uniformed excisemen checking bills of passage draw nearer. He turns his head to look at a carriage drawn up* *down the dockside. John Frost and Clio Rickman look worriedly out at him through the window.*

PAINE'S LETTER VOICE: ... A government plot to seize me and drag me to the courts have been narrowly foiled, thanks principally to the efforts of a friend and, so it would seem, a poet called Blake. It's time I was back in France ...

The excisemen check Paine's bill against a list and a letter, step away for some confidential mutters, return to escort him from the line.

PAINE'S VOICE: ... Seems the courts have found me guilty of criminal libel *in absentia* and declared me outlaw. Is it not a dangerous attempt in any government to say to a Nation, "Thou shalt not read"...?

Frost puts on his hat, checks his watch, lowers himself down to the dock, ready for work. Rickman hands him down his cane and case.

Customs Post, *quayside, Dover. Paine stands in a small room, barred windows on two sides, getting back into his clothes. Through one window he can see the boat for France, boarding down to a trickle; through the other, the dockside carriage and, beyond, the approach road to the harbour. A clock ticks remorselessly on a wall above his head. His bags lie on a table, his belongings everywhere. Whistles from outside, gangways being removed. An Exciseman appears in doorway.*

EXCISEMAN: Chief's arrived. Constable's on his way. You're going back to London, me lad ... Ye've a visitor.

He steps aside, moves off to fetch his Chief. Frost burls in, all lawyer. Nods at Paine, checks the dockside window. Paine watches.

PAINE: Don't look good, eh.

FROST: *(Busy checking his notebook)* Sir John Harcourt, the man himself ... *(To Paine)* They reckon a warrant's on its way. For the moment you're held under suspicion of a capital offence ...

PAINE: What, writing a book?

FROST: *(Serious)* Men've swung fer less, Tom. *(Sounds of boots in passageway)* Not a word, all right? I do the barkin'. *(Lifts voice as door swings open)* ... I believe I shall need to put this matter directly to the Attorney-General. *(The Chief appears, the exciseman behind him)* Ah. Am I at last in the presence of the responsible officer, sir?

CHIEF: You are, sir. I do my duty here, nothing more.

FROST: And yer warrant?

CHIEF: Understand it's on its way, sir. Constable's meant to be bringing it down the hill ...

FROST: Hmm. My client, a prominent businessman, well known in the City, stands to lose thousands of poundsworth of business in Holland because you "understand" a warrant is "on its way"...? Look at him. Is that, I ask ye, the face of a criminal ...? *(The two men stare at Paine. He stares back. Frost is back at the window)* I will be plain, sir, time is money. If ye would care to join me at this window, ye will see the coach I came in. *(The Chief shuffles a little, uncertain)* If ye peer closely, ye might recognise the gentleman who sits within, I see you have a glass there ... (*The Chief reluctantly joins him, peers at the coach through his telescope. Close shot of Rickman, deep in vacancy, picking his nose).* The sixth Baronet of Cuckney, sir, and Presiding Magistrate for this County, and my brother-in-law. *(The Chief lowers the glass, returns to the safety of the doorway. Paine watches on, sees a coach appear at the top of the hill down to the harbour, begin the sharp descent at a clatter.)* Now, unless my client be released at once to board his ship, a warrant for **your** immediate arrest and detention will be in a constable's hand within ten minutes.

Silence. The clock ticks. Final sounds of imminent departure from quayside. Frost checks the window. The speeding coach slows to turn into the docks.

CHIEF: *(Feeling his collar)* We only do our duty, sir ...

FROST: Three words, gentlemen. *(Checks the window. The coach is halfway along the quayside.)* Sir John Harcourt.

The Chief flinches; throws a murderous glare at his luckless exciseman.

Jetty. The boat's some way out from the jetty, moving slowly in the still air. Three lawmen scuttle toward the Customs Post, coach doors left open behind them. Frost and Rickman watch them enter the Post, then emerge moments later to stare after the ship. Rickman turns, waves. Paine stands at the rail, hand raised. Over this,

PAINE'S VOICE: ... Perhaps I'm done with England now, perhaps the book will do, they say one man in ten has read it or heard it read. Thought, by some means or other, is got abroad in the world, and cannot be restrained, though reading may ...

*FRANCE, 1792, Calais Harbour. September evening. A large excited crowd waits for the boat to dock and Paine to show. A band plays revolutionary tunes with some vigour. Officers of the Calais Assembly and other luminaries form an official welcoming party. Banners proclaim their meanings: **Pas de Calais welcomes Thomas Paine; a new Deputy for a new Convention; Long live the Rights of Man**. Over this,*

PAINE'S VOICE ... Reports from France leave my reserves of hope somewhat depleted. Sacking the King was absolutely right, but should have happened a year back, before he had chance to embroil ye in this pointless war with Austria and Prussia, which clearly threatens all ye seek to create ...

Paine arrives on the gangway: music, cheering, vast applause. He smiles; waves.

PAINE'S VOICE: ... The good folk of Calais seek to make amends by electing me *in absentia* Deputy to the new Convention and Honorary Frenchman. English, American, now French, is this a step in the right direction, for one who would be a Citizen of the   World ...?

He reaches quayside kisses, hugs, speeches. Smiles on everything.

Slow fade to black.

PAINE'S VOICE: ... At least no-one here would have me dead.

Paris. *Day. The shot slowly tracks the grounds of the Luxembourg, one-time palace, now prison. Mutilated corpses lie in rough lines across the grass and dirt, some still in their prison chains, the as yet unidentified remnant of brutal massacres. Paine arrives at the heart of the carnage, watches relatives pick their fearful way across the site, seeking their own. A weeping woman claims a husband. Two men heave his legless form into a half-loaded cart. Ox-drawn open carts trundle in and out, bearing the claimed corpses to the burial ground. Smoke from rubbish-pyres thickens the thin autumn haze.*

A Ministry of Justice coach draws up nearby, Danton leaps out to speak with a group of Deputies. Paine turns to leave, face stony, sickened. Hears his name called. Sees Danton leaving the group he's with to come to meet him.

DANTON: Welcome back, Paine. As ye see, sir, the Revolution has not been idle in your absence.

PAINE: Why? *(A sweep of the hand across the killing field)* What does it mean?

DANTON: Waste not good tears, Mr Paine, most of 'em were enemies, when you know the circumstance ...

PAINE: Circumstance? What circumstance on earth can justify the brutal slaughter of thousands of chained prisoners by crazed citizens' death squads, mister, while the Revolution stands by and does **nothing** ...? Where was the Minister of Justice ...?

DANTON: *(Eyeing him; cool)* ... The Prussian Army stood
seventy miles from Paris, the Minister of Justice was
busy raising a People's Militia to up and throw 'em out.
Ten thousand patriots answered the call, eager to go, yes,
but not while the prisons of Paris sat swelled to bursting
with the enemies of their revolution, who might break
out in their absence and take revenge on the undefended
families our patriot volunteers would leave behind.
(Sweeps a hand at the killing field) They did what they
did. I turned my back. I was busy saving the Revolution.
(They eye each other. Paine takes deep breaths; reeling)
Paine, there's no maps cover the place we've got to or
the land ahead. Stay close, friend. Ye could, I promise ye,
do much worse ... *(Inclines his head towards the nearby
group. Paine takes them in; spots the dwarf Marat; the
others strangers, one Robespierre, dabbing a nosegay to
his face; and Bancal)* Be useful here. Take a hand in
writing the new Constitution, lead the Committee, I'll
back ye. But don't get embroiled elsewhere. Especially,
should we decide to proceed with it, in the trial of the
King. This fever must run its course ...

PAINE: Trial, did ye ...?

*He's gone. Paine turns away, bearings gone, grim; takes a
last look at the carnage.*

*Bring up sounds of Convention Hall: a Deputy's voice
votes "**Mort**", to excited applause from public gallery; a
second voice, a third ...*

*High shot of Paine, a loaded cart moving past him. The
cart lurches on. Hacked bodies twitch and bob their way
to burial.*

Salle de Manège. *A line of Deputies queue to voice their
vote at the podium. The line stretches from entrance hall to
President's tribune, most of it inching slowly forward
through a curtained-off hospitality zone annexed for
Deputies and guests. Up ahead, unseen, each vote voiced
receives vociferous response from Assembly and Galleries.*

*We reach Paine, on line in the hospitality area. The space buzzes: food, drink and cordials are served at tables; wives, mistresses and hired 'actresses' in négligés mingle in the moil of deputies and dignitaries. A book on the outcome does brisk business by the door. The Bookies' talleyman chalks up a rough running total of votes cast in two columns: **Mort** and **Pas Mort**. Paine watches impassively. A Deputy up ahead votes for Imprisonment; hissing, voiced anger from unseen Gallery and Deputies' benches; the talleyman chalks up another **Pas Mort**. A House Usher enters the screened area, reads out another list of deputies to join the line. Several tables begin to clear.*

Paine scans the place, looking for someone. Sees Danton wave to him from a crowd of guests, many of them 'actresses' and businessmen. Paine nods back, catches sight of his contact entering from the hall proper.

BANCAL: *(Arriving; around 40; Secretary to the Convention)* Good, I'm in time. You would vote in French, yes? Let me see it *(Paine hands him a slip of paper. Bancal frowns, flicks a look at Paine, pencils in the translation, hands it back.)* You're quite sure about this, sir? *(Paine nods)* I'm there if ye need me. But slow, eh? And clear. In there it is circus ...

He leaves for the Convention Hall proper. Paine wipes sweat from his face and neck, prepares for the ordeal ahead, the line threading through a screen doorway into the main hall. Hears his name called behind him, sees Carnet hand Benjamin to a companion and cross to join him. Paine moves slowly towards her through the mill of people. They stand in silence for a moment, eyes on eyes.

CARNET: Ye should not have come back, Paine.

PAINE: No choice.

CARNET: Things will not be the same now. Do not involve yourself in this ...

PAINE: Can't see a way out. In any case, country needs a constitution, I help write it ...

CARNET: Ye're a stubborn man. *(He looks away, then back, her gaze unwavering.)* I hoped ye would write me.

PAINE: I wrote ye. Plenty. Didn't send 'em.

The line moves. He notes it.

CARNET: I'm where I was. If ye need help.

He nods. Watches her up the stairs to the Visitors Galleries, moves in through the screened door to resume his place on line. The utterly changed Assembly hits him full face: two packed galleries, the left crammed with Workers' Sections, the Right with wigs and britches; the floor seething with tension, deputies calling abuse from their party stations. High and to the left sits the radical Mountain: low and to the right, the liberal Gironde, the government party; across the centre, outnumbering both, the independent/opportunist Plain.

A great swell of applause rises from the left as the Mountain high command approach the podium.

BARÈRE: Citizen Robespierre.

A slim, stiff, short man, early thirties, climbs the steps, skyblue satin coat, creamyellow britches, powdered wig, nosegay in one hand, kerchief in the other. Receives sustained, respectful greeting from the gallery and elsewhere in calm, impassive silence.

ROBESPIERRE: *(Eventually; the lips barely move)* Robespierre, on behalf of the nameless millions who have suffered the cruelty of kings, votes Death to this one.

He leaves the podium to heavy applause, which swells to excited cheering and stamping as Barère names:

BARÈRE: Citizen Marat.

Bedlam. Women scream his name: Blessed Marat, Friend of the People; frenzy, mania, edging towards psychopathy, shift the show to new levels of feeling.

Paine's face, watching the weird ape-like midget take the podium, five feet nothing of swarthy charisma and rampant psoriasis, trousers and open shirt à la Sansculotte, hair everywhere, a pair of pistols stuffed into his waist-sash. The Mountain has stood as one to applaud; the governing Right sits stonily on its hands; the Centre's indifferent or amused. Marat sucks deep on the adulation, big eyes bulging from the Swiss-Italian face; at length raises an index finger to his lips for order; gets it at once.

MARAT: Marat, Friend of the People. Let the guillotine sing for this murderous King. Death. Death. Death ...

The Workers' Sections thunder "Death", Marat returns to the floor, stands theatrically before his adulators. Barère gavels for order. Marat begins to cackle, his Gallery supporters join in. Marat begins to head back to his seat on the Mountain; stops to look as he hears Paine's name called; Paine climbs the podium. Checks Bancal's scrawl on his slip of paper. The place waits to hear him.

PAINE: *(In French)* Thomas Paine. I vote for imprisonment until the war with Austria and Prussia ends, exile thereafter.

Mutters, as people try to deal with his French. Calls go up: "What did he say? Repeat, repeat". Barère, this month's President, repeats Paine's words, jeers and hisses lift uncertainly from the Workers' Sections, a ripple of approval from Right and Centre, both tailing quickly off.

Paine returns to the floor. Sees Danton shaking his head at him. Heads for an empty front row bench in the centre, directly in the President Barère's eye-line. Secretary Bancal, at a raised desk on the President's right, nods a greeting.

Barère closes the roll, rings his summoning bell, ushers take it up around the hall, calling absent Deputies to their seats. Bancal works at the President's side on the tally sheets. The hall resumes a tense, rather eery silence.

Danton approaches Paine's bench. Gazes around the hall, acknowledging others, as he speaks sotto voce, as if passing the time of day.

DANTON: Paine. Take this matter no further, ye only harm yourself, those who lead the Mountain will soon lead the country and, as ye see, the Mountain asks Death. I speak as a true friend.

He moves off; climbs to resume his seat at Marat's right hand, Robespierre on Marat's left. Ushers close and bar the Hall's doors. The President stands, rings his bell, tally sheet in hand.

BARÈRE: The votes cast are as follows: For imprisonment and exile - 288 votes. For death with clemency - 72 votes. Total against death - 360. *(Long Pause)* For death without qualification - 361.

Barère looks up from the sheet. The hall sits on in deep, odd silence, on the edge of history. A solitary voice, Marat's, calls a single word from the Mountain: "Death". The Gallery cracks into life, the chant spreads, deepens. The King's lawyers rise from their table, Malesherbes in the lead, begin to leave the hall. The President bells order, ushers clack at galleries and benches, Paine looks across at a Government Deputy who sits weeping, face in his hands.

BARÈRE: *(A note in his hand)* One moment, citizens. I have in my hand a technical motion for reprieve put down earlier by Citizen Brissot on behalf of the governing faction ... *(Over the fury)* Will you speak, Citizen?

Brissot, the weeping Deputy near Paine, sits upright, wipes his face, shakes his head. Paine rises, Barère sees him. Frowns. The house stills. Barère whispers to Bancal.

BANCAL: *(In English)* The President asks if you have a motion, Citizen?

Paine nods.

BARÈRE: The chair recognizes Citizen Paine, Deputy for the Pas de Calais.

Uproar again from Workers' Sections in the Gallery. The death-chant sets up again. Paine crosses to the podium, Bancal gets down to follow him. En route, Paine feels the stares of the Mountain; sees Danton watching, shaking his head.

Paine waits, grim-faced, as President and ushers seek order; scans the public galleries; spots Carnet and De Bonneville, Benjamin in his arms, watching him.

PAINE: *(Eventually; Bancal translating, a step below him)* The decision reached today in favour of death fills me with genuine sorrow, friends. When I go home to America, perhaps to write a history of these days, I would find more joy in recounting a multitude of mistakes prompted by compassion than in recording one act, however just, grounded in severity ...

MARAT: *(Up and screaming)* Quaker, Quaker, Quaker, Quaker.

PAINE: *(Turns on him fast)* ... No, mister, I am not a Quaker, never have been, ye shame yourself and insult this Convention with your wind and whistle ...

Tumult. Paine waits, white with it, bridges already half burned. The Governing Faction are on their feet applauding him, the Mountain's volcanically shouting him down. Bancal's hands tremble on the stair-rail.

BARÈRE: *(Eventually, as a sort of order's regained)* Your motion, Citizen ...

PAINE: *(Nodding to translating Bancal)* Citizens, for the first time in history, the system of monarchy has been **abolished**. If we need to mark this giant's step in human history, let us smash the crown of gold into a million pieces and throw them into the air that each man and woman in the land may have a piece; for thus we will show all of suffering humanity that here, in France, it is the people who have become sovereign. But I ask ye, in whose interest do we now seek to exterminate the pathetic mutt that remains, that ill-reared wreck of a man, the last Louis? I tell ye plain, friends. The enemies of France, the enemies of liberty and humanity, the enemies of the new spirit of revolution, pray fervently for this King's death. How can it be in our interest to give them the pretext they seek to wage a Holy War on all we mean to create here? I move suspension. I move for Life

Concerted shouting has broken out on the Mountain. Paine climbs down. The hall's been scattered, defocused; ripples of applause and hooting drift into silence. Barère looks at the Mountain. Robespierre has risen in his place. Barère names him.

ROBESPIERRE: *(Simply)* Let the sentence be pronounced, let the enemy within and without understand it: we will be masters in our own house ...

We have watched Paine a great deal of the time, head in hands, Bancal's lips close to his ear. He sits up stonefaced as the applause thunders out. Knows he's lost. Scans the galleries. Sees Carnet watching him.

Fade sound.

Bring up sustained drum roll.

Place de la Révolution. *A blade hisses down. Zunk. Paine's face in the crowd, eyes closed. Shouts of **Vive la Nation**. The Marseillaise sets up. Paine turns away, moves.*

Edge of Place de la Révolution, wrapped in mist, Paine emerging from the great crowd. William Short stands at a corner, some distance from a black carriage bearing the US seal, looking out for him. Calls Paine. Paine approaches, they shake hands, exchange a muttered word or two. Paine studies the coach a moment.

PAINE: Is he there? *(Short nods, glum)* What's he want? *(Short shrugs)* OK.

Paine heads for the coach. The near door pushes slowly open; a wooden leg appears in the gap; Gouverneur

Morris follows it, crabbing sideways on the seat to speak through the doorway. In the near distance, the execution rituals continue apace, as locks of Louis' hair are auctioned from the scaffold.

GOUVERNEUR MORRIS: My office advises all American citizens to leave without delay. The civilized nations look set to act to put this rabble back in its rightful place and there are bloody times ahead. I cannot be held responsible for the safety of those who wilfully ignore the warning ... I thought ye should know.

PAINE: Aye. I'm obliged.

GOUVERNEUR MORRIS: Understand ye're sought for Criminal Libel and declared an Outlaw back in England ... *(Paine sniffs; nothing)* From now on, if ye've business with my ministry, ye see the Master, not his dog.

Paine steps back. Morris whistles Short to return. Short approaches, boards. Morris draws the door to.

PAINE: One thing, mister. Does your appointment mean our country washes its hands of France now ...?

Morris stares at him darkly for a moment; bangs the roof with his canehead; the coach rumbles off. Paine watches it drift into the mist. Crowd sounds rise, fall back, fade to mute.

Committee Room, *Convention Building. Late winter. The huge committee table groans under the weight of learned books of reference, articles, journals and drafts. Sixteen men sit around it, voting their draft Constitution clause by clause. Paine, with Bancal at his side, chairs the session and calls the votes. All sixteen pen their initials on each clause passed. Outside, a steady pulse of snow, turning the room gradually darker. Over this,*

PAINE'S LETTER VOICE: My dear Jefferson, We are now in an extraordinary crisis, and it is not without some considerable faults here ...

Faubourg St Denis*. Late Spring. Rambling country
mansion house; Paine's first-floor, three-room apartment,
overlooking courtyard and rear garden.*

*Paine writes at a desk by a window over yard and garden.
We see an envelope, already addressed, by his left hand;
read "Thomas Jefferson Esq, Secretary of State,
Washington". Sounds of livestock drift up from below.*

PAINE'S LETTER VOICE: ... The new Constitution I came
here to help draft lies unacknowledged, gathering dust.
Not long ago I felt there was a good chance of
extending liberty through the greatest part of Europe;
but I now relinquish that hope and begin to
contemplate returning home ...

*A squawking below draws his eyes to the yard. Carnet
and the two year old Benjamin just arrived at the back
gate: random geese, duck, turkey panic as the toddler gets
amongst them. Paine steps out onto a small metal stair-
head covered in vine, stares down at the still lass below,
who's asking Paine's whereabouts of the landlord down
the yard.*

PAINE: Here.

Carnet looks up, sees him.

CARNET: S'beautiful here.

PAINE: Aye. Put a few shillings away from the last book ...

*The landlord carries a basket of corn for the birds; takes
Benjamin in tow. Shows him several rabbits, two pigs in a
pen. Carnet climbs the stair; Paine steps back to let her
by, follows her into the workroom. She dwells at the
window desk a moment, lays a package down on it.
Paine's eyes follow her carefully.*

PAINE: S'that?

CARNET: S'your *Open Letter to the Convention*.

*She passes down the room and into the next, examining his
new quarters. Paine empties his manuscript from the*

package. Stares at it. She returns to stand in the far doorway. Paine looks at her inquiringly, the manuscript in his hand.

CARNET: The Group discussed it . We don't feel able to print it. I'm sorry.

Paine nods. Lays it down. Examines his ink-stained hands.

PAINE: Your ... friends don't agree with me, is that it?

She shakes her head, crosses to the side window, rests her head on the frame, wan, unhappy.

CARNET: Danton sent word we'd been denounced by some of the militant sections. "Hostile to the Revolution", they dub us ... Journals that oppose the coming Terror and the Coming Men behind it tend to find their shops attacked and their presses smashed to pieces. We lie low for a time.

Benjamin shrieks with glee down in the yard, as a goose pecks corn from his palm. They watch him a moment through their separate windows.

PAINE: He's a sweet boy. *(She nods, says nothing)* Did ye eat? I have some eggs. Will I make some eggs ...?

She smiles, fond. He passes into the next room, removes his shirt, pours water into a bowl, preparing to wash.

PAINE: We'll take a meal together. I'd like that.

She watches a moment through the open arch, as he swills his lean hard frame with water. Moves into the room he's in. Sits to watch and be with him.

CARNET: What'll ye do then?

PAINE: Well, if you'd agree to put it into French for me, I guess I could have a stab at just ... reading it out myself in the Convention hall ...

CARNET: Oh Paine, Paine. Ye think Marat, Robespierre, Danton are gonna stand for that? They don't want yer Constitution, not until they run things anyway, when they can rewrite it for themselves ... Can ye not see the danger?

He turns, wash done, towel in hand. They look at each other quietly for some moments.

PAINE: Yes, I see the danger.

CARNET: Ye have the body of a boy still. The innocence too. Come ...

He approaches her, she takes the towel, begins to dry his body. He flinches as she touches the kidney area.

CARNET: What?

He shakes his head. She looks more closely: the slicing cut he took from the Sansculotte assault stands proud from the skin, poorly healed.

CARNET: Did I not say it needed potash?

She reaches her head forward, kisses the scar very gently. His hands hover about her head uncertainly, delicately stroke the pale hair.

PAINE: I'm old, Carnet.

CARNET: *(Small shake of head)* You're the youngest man I ever knew.

Long shot from work room of the couple, melded in the sunlit space beyond. He draws her slowly upright from the stool. She lifts her eyes to him. They hold on to each other, silent, on the edge of something.

BENJAMIN'S VOICE: *(Sudden, close)* Voilà, maman!

She turns to look. Benjamin stands at the stair-head door, a day-old chick cupped in his hands.

CARNET: Bravo, petit. Bravo.

She leaves Paine's arms, stoops to hug the boy. Paine watches. Fade sound; bring up the bells of Paris, sounding the tocsin. Trail Paine's voice, rehearsing aloud his projected address in French, en route to the Convention Hall.

162

Moving carriage. Early summer day. Carnet sits opposite Paine, Benjamin on her knee, helping Paine struggle through her French translation of his Open Letter to the Convention, her attention shifting increasingly to the action in the streets beyond the window. The bells grow louder, more menacing.

PAINE: *(Looking up from page)* What is it? D'ye know?

She shakes her head. The carriage stops as folk swirl across the roadway, Carnet calls to a group of National Guards stationed at a corner, they rap out a curt answer, the coach moves on. Carnet sits back, teeth working worriedly on upper lip.

PAINE: What?

CARNET: The Workers' Sections rise again. They have the Convention hall surrounded. Some are already inside with guns and a list of demands ... Looks like the Coming Men are come.

Paine stares out at the streets a moment, bangs his stick-head on the roof, the coach draws up again. They sit in silence for a moment.

CARNET: Paine. Don't.

PAINE: Take the boy home.

He reaches for the door, she puts her hand on his wrist.

CARNET: What can ye do? Mm?

He shakes his head, bleak-eyed; steps out of the coach. Heads off on foot. Carnet watches him out of sight. The coachman appears at the window for instruction.

BENJAMIN: Chez nous, citoyen.

Tuileries. Convention Building. We follow Paine moving through a thickening silent crowd of Parisians staring at the Convention Hall. We see him emerge beyond the limits of the throng, cross a no-man's land of grass, approach the stone-flagged terrace. National Guard, squads of armed workers from the Sections, hundreds of provincial volunteers surround the Building. Twelve cannons have been strategically placed around it, aimed at the Hall. Flags and banners proclaim the aims of the rising: 'Insurrection et Vigeur'; 'À bas les Girondistes'; 'Immurez les ministres'; 'Tirez le mauvais sang de Brissot et les traîtres'; 'À la lanterne avec les speculateurs et les amasseurs'; 'Sauvez la Revolution' ...

Paine crosses the terrace, headed for the great doors to the Grand Concourse. Sees Bancal and several other white-faced Deputies coming out.

BANCAL: *(Angry, fearful)* ... The insurgents've sealed the doors to the Chamber, they let no one in and no one out until their demands are voted through ...

PAINE: What is it they ask?

BANCAL: Everything. And at once. Mainly they want Brissot and his whole Cabinet arrested ...

PAINE: This is not revolution, this is anarchy ...

He heads on for the door.

BANCAL: (Calling) Paine ...

Paine pushes in to the Grand Concourse. Silent soldiery and worker militants stand at the ready facing the entrance-ways into the Chamber. Small sounds echo eerily round the empty space. A young officer bars his way just inside the door. Paine produces his Convention pass; the young man studies it a moment, salutes him, calls down the Concourse. A senior officer detaches from a huddle by the main Hall doors, heads up the marble in their direction. Paine recognises him as a Danton man: Hanriot. The young man nods Paine forward.

The two men meet in the centre of the Concourse. Paine hands him his pass, watches the hard-faced Hanriot study it; asks if he speaks any English. Hanriot says nothing for some moments, then looks at him.

HANRIOT: A little, citoyen. *(Hands him back the pass)* This is not of use here today. You take it home, make ... *(Mimes curling his hair)* ... in hair with it ...

PAINE: I see. And on whose authority do you keep an elected Deputy from his work ...?

Hanriot frowns, working it out; draws a pistol from his waistband; points it carefully at Paine's head.

HANRIOT: His.

Paine squints at the barrel of the gun.

VOICE: *(Lifted)* Hanriot! Calme-toi, calme-toi ...

Hanriot smiles, lowers the pistol. Danton burls up from the conference by the door. A brief exchange in French, Hanriot recedes back to the huddle.

DANTON: Mr Paine, go home, sir. If ye value your life at all, lie low until this passes ...

PAINE: This your doing, Danton ...?

Danton takes Paine's arm, moves him carefully towards an alcove beneath the stairs to the Galleries.

DANTON: I will answer your question, but I beg ye not to stand in full public view like this ... *(Low voice, tense, wired)* It is not my doing, sir, but I **am** trying to control the outcome ...

PAINE: D'ye have access to the Hall?

DANTON: I do.

PAINE: Will ye help me get in?

DANTON: In? Are ye mad? Why?

PAINE: We've had a draft Constitution gathering dust on a shelf for half a year, I helped write the damn thing, I move we implement it. Today, if possible. *(Danton listens, wide-eyed with disbelief)* Listen, without a constitution there is no law, without law there is no Revolution ... *(Danton frowns, impatient. Paine's voice lifts)* Let this continue *(Waves a hand at the scene in the concourse)* we end up with whoever has the guns making the rules and in my book that's tyranny and I want no part of it, mister.

The great doors bang open at the other end of the Concourse, Marat and Robespierre advance on the cluster of National Guard and Worker Militants. Marat squeals something to Hanriot, who calls several squads of soldiers to form up facing the doors.

DANTON: *(Sotto)* The First Minister and his Cabinet plan to march out ...

Silence. Paine watches the appalling scene; fixes on Robespierre, who stands a little apart from the others, still, calm, watchful.

DANTON: *(In his ear; apropos Robespierre)* May the good Lord save us from those who would save us ...

The Marseillaise sets up inside the Hall. The doors bang open again. Brissot appears at the head of a column of singing Deputies, fifty maybe. Hanriot orders his men to take aim. The column stops; the song shrivels on their lip. Brissot throws out a shaky question; Hanriot gives a terse answer. A slow, stubborn argument ensues.

DANTON: Paine, keep away from this place. On the page I give you no argument, but men are flesh and blood, not paper and ink, a Revolution cannot be made on rosewater. This government is corrupt, incompetent, they hang on and hang on while the country groans, the people are right to throw them out and put us in their stead. You'll see. But from now on it is we who will have to take the terrible measures, so that the people do not take them themselves ...

He begins to move away.

PAINE: *(Quietly)* **State** terror, ye mean ...?

Danton turns. Just as quiet.

DANTON: We ride a tiger, sir.

He makes a biting gesture with his great mouth. Heads off down the marble, calling advice to Brissot and the Cabinet men as he goes, his huge voice swelling and wobbling round the Concourse. Brissot begins to answer, Hanriot takes out his pistol, calmly fires it at the ceiling. The demonstrating Deputies scatter at once back into the hall. Marat claps his hands in manic glee. Plaster and dust fall gauzily onto the marble floor.

Paine turns away. Slumps onto a banquette behind him. Lays his head back, eyes closed, hand to his sore side, as if he'd taken the shot himself.

Close shot of his face: like a death mask, terminus reached. Laughter from down the Concourse.

Fade sound. Bring up drum roll.

A guillotine flashes downward: zunk. Slowed motion of a severed head twirling down towards the waiting basket. It lands face up: Brissot stares up at us, eyes still open.

Avenue. *Autumn night. Paine walks slowly along an avenue of gaunt Lombardy poplars, deep in himself; gradually becomes aware of the clop of a following coach, some metres behind him; senses he's being followed; pulls into the trees, unflaps his britches, as if to piss. The coach draws on a little, stops some metres beyond him. Silence. Paine watches, tense. A young man steps out, looks back at him.*

MAN: Mr Paine? Mr Paine, s'Will Short ...

Paine blinks. Buttons up. Approaches the coach.

PAINE: S'goin' on, Will ...?

SHORT: Forgive me, I needed to be sure ye weren't followed before I spoke with ye . Will we ride, sir?

Paine studies the young man's drawn face, worried eyes.

The coach clips at pace through parkland. Inside it, Paine gazes at a document in his hand.

PAINE: What is it, boy?

SHORT: S'a passport. Belonged to one of our sea captains held up by the British blockade. Died of the fever in Le Havre, I lifted it from the files.

Paine sniffs, closes the passport. Shakes his head. Hands it back.

SHORT: Morris has had three meetings about ye with members of the Committee for Public Safety, I've seen his notes, they look to charge ye under the Law of Enemy Aliens or the Law of Suspects. *(Silence. Paine broods)* It's not all. *(He opens the second document: a letter; hands it to him)* Remember writing this to Mr Jefferson?

Long silence. Paine looks down at the letter.

PAINE: *(Numb)* Go on.

SHORT: God knows how many others they've intercepted, they brought that one round last week, wanted Morris to verify the signature, Morris was away, I said I'd look to it ...

Paine shakes his head bleakly. Hands the letter back. Stares out at the night. Short leans forward to replace the passport on Paine's lap.

SHORT: *(Quietly)* Ye've much work t'accomplish, Mr Paine. I could not bear to see that great head of yours in a basket ...

Paine opens his eyes, looks across at him. Pockets the passport. Closes eyes again.

PAINE: Tired o' leggin' it round the world, Willie. Tryin' to tek root. But I thank ye, sir. Ye're a good un.

Faubourg St Denis. *Night. Paine watches Short's carriage roll away into the dark, enters the courtyard of* *the St. Denis house, jolts to a halt, mid-pace, eyes raised to his apartment windows. Small lamps burn in each of his three rooms. He pulls back to the courtyard wall, hunkers down between a pair of rabbit hutches to watch.*

His face, dealing with eventualities, the realness of things joltingly present, for a moment draining him of hope. Rabbits twitch at wire beside him; suggest the future.

A flick of a human form passes a window; a long thrown shadow in adjoining room; then stillness, nothing.

He breathes deep, gathering resolve.

He stands on the vine-clad outside stairhead, peers in at the empty front work-room. Listens. Pushes silently in. Takes in the room, edges slowly through arch into utility room. Inches sideways, back to wall, towards part-open door to bedroom. Tiny sounds from within. He places a finger on the door, glides it, bit by bit, ajar. Sees a bright wood fire in the grate; Carnet dozing on the rug before the hearth, her head across a heap of his manuscript pages; the table laid for cold supper, a pair of wine bottles, corks eased.

Paine stands a moment, head back against wall, regathering. Blows held air from taut lungs. Crosses to fireside, crouches to free trapped pages from her pale strewn hair. Her eyes blink open suddenly, give him a fierce stare, like some small night-animal's.

PAINE: S'me.

He resumes collecting the manuscript. She sits up.

CARNET: Robespierre denounced the foreign deputies at the Jacobins this evening ...

PAINE: *(Busy)* What, all of 'em ...?

CARNET: Ahunh. But you by name. *(Beat)* I came to warn ye. *(He sniffs; nods)* I didn't know where ye were, I waited on. I thought they might have taken you in.

PAINE: I was walkin'.

He carries the manuscript into the front work-room, sits at his desk to address an envelope to Clio Rickman in London, places the text inside and seals it. Carnet has followed him; watches him in silence from the arch.

PAINE: ... Called at the Cordeliers t'see the Great Murdered Martyr Marat lyin' in state. Pantomime, obscene pan ...

CARNET: Are ye mad? Why, why d'ye provoke them so? You act as if ye're free to say and do what you please.

PAINE: No. I just act as if I ought to be. *(Taps the envelope)* I shall need this sending to London, will ye do it for me?

Silence. They stare on at each other across the dark space.

CARNET: You aim to stay on here, don't ye. *(No answer)* Why? D'ye know y'self?

He broods a moment, eyes still on hers. Shakes his head.

PAINE: I used t'agree with Mr Franklin: where there is liberty, there is my country, Here, now, I feel it different ... where there is not liberty, there is mine. These people and their senseless Terror hurl us headlong into but another tyranny, it's they who're wrong, not me. I'll sit until they shift me.

He sniffs. Shrugs. She shakes her head, saddened.

PAINE: *(Low voice)* But I'm glad ye came, Carney.

CARNET: The new book is very fine. *(He nods; thanks)* I also read yer letters from England. *(He looks at her)* The ones ye didn't send. I'd love t'have bin there when ye read 'em to yer horse. *(He smiles; looks away)* Ye hungry?

PAINE: I'm hungry.

CARNET: I thought we might have that meal together.

He nods. Smiles. She peels back towards the bedroom. He stands, empties his greatcoat pockets onto the desk, sees the sea-captain's passport in among the bits and pieces, looks at it a moment, as he removes the coat.

Bedroom. *He sits at table, watching her uncork the second bottle, pour their drinks. A town clock sets up, strikes midnight, some way away.*

PAINE: S'the boy cared for?

CARNET: De Bonneville has him. He knows I'm here.

She lifts her glass. He joins her.

PAINE: What? The future?

CARNET: *(A headshake)* The future lies in an alley with its throat cut. Tonight.

He frowns. They click glasses. Sip. Carnet carries hers to the hearth, kneels to stare at the fire, her back to him.

PAINE: Nay, lass. That's despair talkin' ...

CARNET: ... We leave for Holland the day after tomorrow. De Bonneville, Benjamin, me. In Amsterdam we have friends, a press, we can work there until it's safe to come home.

Long silence. Paine watches her still head, pale hair shimmered by flame; deals with his feelings: love, fear, age, loneliness.

CARNET: De Bonneville and I married this morning. To ease passage across the frontier. There are but these hours, Paine. I will not toast a future that has you in it only as a grave to be tended ...

He crosses to the hearth, crouches by her side. Tears grease her face; she stays fierce, proud; will not look at him.

PAINE: Carney, Carney, Carney ... *(He pushes his head forward, kisses her pale neck very gently)* How I will miss ye, girl ...

She turns, stares at him.

CARNET: *(A whisper)* Show me. Show me.

171

Bedroom. Oblique imagic tendrils of lovemaking through the night: fierce, direct, honest. Clothing litters the floor; the fire dies slowly in the grate; wine lies in a bloody puddle, spilt from a tumbled glass. In one image, he covers her naked body, head to foot, with words: she laughs her wonderment; in another, she sits astride him, caressing him in French as he moves inside her ...

Front work-room. *Morning. Carnet sits at the desk, writing him a letter. In the bedroom, Paine sleeps on the narrow mattress. Carnet carries the note to the bedroom. Lays it on the pillow by his hand. Runs a finger very gently along his wrist. Leaves.*

The shot moves in on the sleeping Paine, her letter beside him.

December, 1793. *Milky, half-dream-like images of Paine's arrest and imprisonment, bound together by her letter. We see him taken from the house by six arresting officers in bonnets rouges; jammed in a carriage with them, headed for the Luxembourg; the carriage entering the great grey prison courtyard; standing in a reception room, having his satchel searched; marched down a long bleak corridor to the cells. Over this,*

CARNET'S LETTER VOICE: I pray, against hope, that you are spared. Not only that I may see and hold and hear and love you again, but because the world without your awkward, stubborn, tender soul will be a poorer place for us all. I travel as Mme de Bonneville now, but as I leave, I remain, your very true Carnet.

A final image: Paine asleep under his greatcoat on a straw mattress. His face. The cell doors bang open: a voice calls his name; his eyes open.

Luxembourg Prison. *Corridor. Two warders walk Paine along it. A glimpse of condemned men, arms bound behind them, shirt-collars rolled down, hair shorn at the nape, being bundled through an open doorway to waiting tumbrils in the courtyard.*

Interview Room. A guard's fist bangs on an oak door. The door's pushed open. A man sits at a desk at the far end of the large room, poring over a document file; on Paine's approach he looks up, unsmiling; checks his watch: Gouverneur Morris.

GOUVERNEUR MORRIS: I have little time, Paine, ye'll forgive my bluntness. My ... advice, if ye will take it, is to stay calm and draw as little attention to yourself as possible. Any attempt, on your part or my own, to bring your case to public notice, can only serve to remind the powers-that-be of the threat ye apparently pose them.

PAINE: Ye'll do nothing, that it? Is this private malice or American policy ...?

GOUVERNEUR MORRIS: Ye may rest assured, sir. Mr Washington has been fully informed. The President is quite happy to leave your future in my hands, Mr Paine.

Paine dwells a moment, taking it in. Strides to the door. Bangs for the guards.

PAINE: *(Quietly)* Seems a high price to pay for a few mis-spellings and an inadequate grasp o' grammar, mister ...

The guards throw the door open, Paine strides out into the corridor.

Luxembourg Prison courtyard. *Late winter, thin snow. A small group of inmates, men and women, trudge in single file around the exercise yard. At one end, cordoned off by thick rope, six tumbrils are being loaded with bound Sansculottes en route for the block. Paine watches as he walks, conversing with the man behind him.*

PAINE: See anyone ye know, Bancal?

BANCAL: Danton folk. Word is he's resigned his post. Grown sick o' the carnage, they say.

PAINE: Mm. Right but late, I'd say.

*The men ascend the cart; all of them present and active
during the attack on the Convention. Paine stops to watch
them. A red-bonnet guard shouts the line to keep moving.
Paine trudges on.*

Luxembourg prison cell. *Night. Window, lit by small
lamp inside the cell. Odd, snipping sound from within.
The shot creeps down the wet stone wall to Paine's pen, at
work on the page; moves to reveal Bancal on his mattress,
reading a book; adjusts finally to the source of the
snipping: Anarcharsis Cloots, on a chair by the cell door,
having his dense black hair shorn by the prison barber,
his shirt collar already ripped out.*

*The barber finishes; holds up a punctilious mirror for
Cloots. Cloots giggles at the gesture. The barber bangs on
the door, a guard lets him out. Paine lays down his pen.*

CLOOTS: I do not understand ... anything. They call me
enemy. They call me enemy ...

*A bell sounds in the pasageway. Doors smash open,
voiced instructions, men protesting. Paine approaches
Cloots, embraces him gently.*

PAINE: I saw ye at the Cordeliers my first visit here. Ye
were something to remember.

*The door cracks open, guards move in to bind his hands
behind him, lead him off. The door's slammed to. Paine
and Bancal exchange a sombre stare. Cloots's voice sets up
outside in the passage: The Marseillaise. Others join him.*

*Prison Cell. Night. Moonlit. Bancal sleeps. Paine lies on
his back on the mattress, watching a spider work a web
across a corner of the ceiling. Footsteps in passageway.
His eyes shift, grow tense. A key in the lock, the door
pushed open, a guard scans the room with a lamp, holds
on Paine.*

GUARD: Venez. Vite.

*Paine gets up slowly, struggles into his coat, gathers his
shoes: his turn.*

GUARD: Laissez-les. (Takes shoes from him, throws them on the mattress) Allez-y.

Paine steps past him into the passageway. Bancal stirs, calls 'Paine ..."

GUARD: Taisez-vous.

Door closed again, locked.

The guard pushes Paine, hands bound behind him, across the dank vastness of the prison. A final door reached. The guard unlocks the great door, pushes Paine through, turns to relock it. Paine surveys the dark vast one-time reception room, bare save for a score or so of specially constructed iron cages lining the two long walls: a sort of death row, the holding area for those about to die.

PAINE: *(Suddenly)* Wait on, ye bastard, I ain't had my trial yet.

The guard lays a huge hand across his mouth, his eyes fierce, lays a knife at his throat.

GUARD: Silence.

He pushes Paine along the gallery of cages, crammed with prone shadowy forms. Holds up at the last cage, shines his lamp on its solitary occupant, who sits inside a blanket, head down.

GUARD: *Voilà.*

The man lifts his head: Danton. He sees Paine; grins. The guard opens the cage, pushes Paine inside.

GUARD: *Deux minutes ...*

DANTON: *Oui oui. Eh. Ses mains ...*

The guard loosens Paine's bindings, relocks the cage, lays down his lamp, retires down the room. Danton's produced a flask of brandy, pours a wooden beaker for each of them, motions him to join him. They squat side by side.

DANTON: *(Voice cracked, shattered)* It's my last night on this good earth, I wanted to spend it with a friend ...

PAINE: S'bad news, boy. I was kinda countin' on ye winnin'...

DANTON: Me too.

He crackles hoarsely. Paine chuckles with him.

DANTON: The revolution ends up eating her own, Paine, eh? *(Silence. They gaze at the beakers in their hands.)* "Aye, but to die, and go we know not where, To lie in cold obstruction till we rot ..."

PAINE: S'that?

DANTON: Shakespeare.

PAINE: S'good.

DANTON: Such a waste.

PAINE: Aye.

DANTON: Some things I will miss. Wet earth. Sweat on a horse's back. Cheesecake at the *Procope*. The sweet tender cunt of my new wife ... *(The guard looms at the bars)* Oui, un moment, citoyen. *(The man withdraws again)* We toast something, eh? You say it. Make me laugh.

PAINE: *(After thought)* The future?

Danton looks at him; begins to laugh.

DANTON: The future. Why not.

They touch, swig. The guard's back. Paine stands. Danton follows him up.

DANTON: Paine. Stay alive. Try to. To the Terror everyone's a carcase. I should know, I created it. Outlive 'em, sir.

PAINE: See what I can do.

He leaves the cage. The guard relocks it. Holds out his hand for Danton's coins. Paine watches the payment.

PAINE: I imagined he did it for love, a secret follower ...

DANTON: Something else I will miss, Paine. Your terrible innocence ...

The guard rebinds Paine's arms, prods him away. Paine cranes for a last look. Danton raises his beaker to him through the bars.

The tocsin sounds out menacingly across the city.

Luxembourg Prison grounds. *High summer. A slow high scan of its several courtyards, busy processing the Terror. At one end, carriages and coaches pour in to disgorge the swelling numbers of newly arrested men; at the other, tumbrils load up with the shorn, headed for the block; between, the space shrunken, the already confined take their daily exercise.*

The shot closes slowly on a barred prison window at ground level. Paine's voice, fevered mumbling; Bancal's, calming him.

Paine's cell. Bancal crouches by Paine's mattress, Paine burbles, in delirium.

PAINE: They ring the bell, what does it mean ...?

Paine's face, neck, rolling in sweat. His eyes open, stare at Bancal.

BANCAL: Hush, hush. I don't know.

PAINE: It is the people. Tyger, tyger, burning bright ...

The door's unlocked, a guard and a doctor push in, Bancal surrenders his place by Paine, the doctor kneels to examine the sick man: head, neck, pulse. He strips the blanket down, Paine's clothing's running sweat. Opens his shirt to feel the stomach; sees, where the scar had been, a fist-sized ulcer, vivid, suppurant; studies it, lips pursed. Stands, wipes his hands, gives instructions to a guard; a second guard joins them, they lay a blanket at the side of the mattress, begin to roll Paine onto it.

The doctor leads the two guards through prison corridors,

Paine slung between them on the blanket-stretcher. Tocsin still heard.

Close shot of Paine's face, eyes opening, closing.

The doctor leads the bearers up a stairway solid with bound and shorn prisoners queuing for the cages. The climb is impeded by the crush, stops are frequent. Paine's eye-view of their faces. Some he recognises: Hanriot, the Danton hardman; others. The bearers reach the open door of the Salle des Cages, are stopped again. Paine stares up at Robespierre, wigless, propped between two guards, his jaw shattered by a bullet, blood drying on his sky-blue coat. For a silent moment they gaze blankly at each other. Robespierre's moved on into the cage-room, the bearers head on for the sick room. The bells stop abruptly.

Prison interview room. *Autumn day. Rain lashes the high barred window. A young man, mid 30s, sits at the desk studying a file of papers. Takes three books from his document case, lays them on the desk: the American, English and French editions of **The Age of Reason 1**. A knock at the door, he looks up with a warm smile, sound of door opening, he stands, the smile fading to shock, concern.*

Paine stands in his greatcoat inside the door. A guard closes it quietly behind him. He's thin, drawn, haggard; his hair lank, largely white.

The young man scans the empty room for a second chair, carries his own around the desk, approaches Paine.

MAN: Mr Paine, sir ... I'm James Monroe, the new American Minister here. Come, ye must sit ...

He leads him to the chair, sees him settled, gathers his file.

MONROE: I'm but recently in post, sir, and did not hear of your detention until two days ago ...

PAINE: D'ye have the date, sir?

MONROE: The date? September 15. *(Pause)* I ... *(Silence. Paine nods)* I must confess I'm somewhat hampered by the ... sparsity of documents left me by my predecessor regarding you, sir ...

PAINE: I bet. Who's in charge out there, d'ye know?

MONROE: For the moment, I believe it's the Convention runs things ... the Revolutionary Government has been toppled, Robespierre, Danton, all gone. It's still a little early to say what new direction's to be taken, though I believe the Terror may well be at an end ...

Paine stands shakily, removes a large manuscript packet from his greatcoat pocket, lays it on the desk.

PAINE: I don't expect much of ye, young man, your office has left me to rot for nigh on a year so I guess that's policy. If ye can see your way to sendin' my new manuscript to Mr Rickman in London, I'll be obliged ...

MONROE: Mr Paine ...

PAINE: Are there still beggars at the gate, sir?

MONROE: *(A frown)* Beggars? I believe there are ...

Paine has removed his greatcoat, lays it on the desk.

PAINE: Give 'em that. Poor days, when a coat outlives a friendship ...

He shambles obdurately for the door. Monroe collects the three books, follows him.

MONROE: *(Resolute)* If I might say one word, sir. *(Paine turns with effort; only anger and hurt hold him together)* I had the honour to meet ye, once at Valley Forge, and again at Rocky Hill ...? Thomas Paine will be freed and soon. Ye have my word on it ...

Paine stands stock-still; looks for words, can't find them.

PAINE: *(Eventually)* Forgive me. I didn't know ye. Give me your hand, boy.

Monroe closes on him, hand out. Paine rests his head on his shoulder a moment.

MONROE: *(Gentle)* There's more, sir ...

He hands Paine the three editions. Paine stares at them. Monroe gently opens the door. Paine shuffles off, books in hand.

Monroe's garden, Paris. *Spring day, warm. A maid moves out from the house, tray in hand; Monroe's wife, young, pretty, follows her. They approach down the garden towards a sunshaded table where a man sits wrapped in a rug, muttering as he works. The maid holds up, Mrs Monroe nods her on; she begins clearing lunch debris as the man works on, chunnering unawares.*

MRS MONROE: And how are ye today, sir?

Paine starts, looks at her.

PAINE: Well, thank ye, Mrs Monroe.

MRS MONROE: There are people arrived to see ye, will I send them down ...?

PAINE: No. Send 'em away.

MRS MONROE: I'll tell them ye're not up to it ...

PAINE: Tell 'em nowt, ma'am. Just send 'em away ...

She nods, a humouring smile, returns to the house. Paine sits back in his chair, stares at the full-blossom apple trees, eyes frosty, some energy returned inside the wanness.

His face, close up. Sounds somewhere, the shriek of a child, his name called, perhaps inside his head. The name again; he turns to look at the house: young Benjamin, pushing five, hurtles down the garden towards him. He stands, the kid almost knocks him over, English and French bubbling from him as they hug and kiss.

Paine looks up at the house again. Carnet stands watching from the terrace, an infant in her arms.

180

Benjamin urges her to come, hurtles off to fetch her, she steps onto the lawn, Paine moves towards her, the kid rushes back onto the grass.

The two meet mid-lawn, beneath a great still-green copper beech, some paces between them; take each other carefully in. The boy whirls around, between, behind them.

CARNET: My God, Paine. Ye really are indestructible.

PAINE: Another boy, is it?

She nods. He holds out his hands, she gives him the sleeping child.

PAINE: What d'ye call this un then?

CARNET: Thomas Paine de Bonneville.

He blinks a look at her. Her gaze is steady. He looks down at the child. Turns away from her.

PAINE: What, miscount your days again?

CARNET: *(Soft)* No, Paine. This time the days were counted.

He ambles off down the garden, eyes steady on the child in his arms.

CARNET: *(Calls after him)* There's room for us all at the old place, if ye'll come ...

He nods vaguely, focus on the bairn. Reaches the apple trees. The kid yawns, stretches, waking; fixes Paine with sharp blue eyes.

PAINE: *(A whisper)* How do, boy.

Benjamin calls him from the terrace. Carnet stands by his work-table, studying his notes. On the terrace, Benjamin calls again, straddling De Bonneville's shoulders. Paine lifts a hand in salute. De Bonneville waves shyly back at him.

CARNET: Will ye come? *(He nods)* Soon?

PAINE: Aye. I'm all but done.

Fade to black

Bring up

PAINE'S LETTER VOICE: Dear Mr President, It is a good while since you asked me to see this thing through; though I have had but indifferent success in the matter, after all these years I believe I may be forgiven for wanting to return to my home ...

Quayside, Le Havre, Summer 1802. *A boat is boarding; Paine sees his baggage stowed. Returns slowly to the gangway, the battered old cowhide satchel on his shoulder.*

PAINE'S LETTER VOICE: ... Since I believe my reputation has sunk somewhat in certain quarters there on account of my book about religion, I will not risk damaging your political standing by seeking a public audience. A private conversation, however, of an hour or two, would gratify me much ...

Paine's slow progress along the quay. He's 65, walks with a stick, upright and lean still, still sturdy. He reaches the gangway. Carnet, mid-thirties, Benjamin (12) and Thomas (8), await him. On deck, the Captain has begun the roll-call. Paine stoops to kiss the two boys, gives them a coin each, stands carefully upright to look at Carnet.

PAINE: Go now. I cannot tek farewells.

CARNET: Within the year ...

He nods. She draws close to him, hugs him tenderly, lays her head on his chest.

PAINE: Go, Carney. It's best.

CARNET: Within the year, Paine.

PAINE: Aye. I hear ye.

He kisses her head very gently. Pushes her away.

PAINE: I'll see you fellers in New York, OK?

182

Benjamin nods.

THOMAS: OK, Paine.

He smiles. Heads off up the gangway. Raises his stick at the top in salute, without looking back. Carnet gathers the kids to her. Stares on at nothing.

At sea. *Fall evening. Slow scan of excited, expectant faces at the ship's rail, gazing out at journey's end. The shot reaches Paine, watching with the rest, eyes hungry for the place.*

NEW YORK, 1802, New York harbour, a low huddle of light on the littoral. His face again.

Quayside. Night. Passengers debarking. A huge crowd gathered below, placards, slogans, banners, lit torches: Ministers of Religion, clerics of one sort and another, Christian Brethren staring up at the gangway in grim silence. A line of police and Sheriff's men hold them in.

Paine appears at top of gangway, the shout goes up, screams of rage and hate split the night, the police line bends, threatens to buckle.

*He begins a slow descent. Below, men run forward carrying tea-chests, empty several hundred copies of his works (principally **The Age of Reason**) into a heap on the quay, torches are handed from the crowd to light them.*

A scan of faces, slogans: Crucify the Anti-Christ; Expel the Loathsome Reptile; Hang the Infamous Scavenger; America loves God; Christ Died For You Too, Paine ... Early Faulwells snarl their Christian message across the dank space, Christ's ayatollahs of the day.

Paine, quayside, walks the gauntlet. Hurled books strike him, spittle runs down his face, mud brought in buckets spatters his clothing. Oaths, imprecations, rage. Police shoulder him through to a waiting carriage. Behind, a hymn sets up, full voiced: All holy Lord, we pray to thee, keep us tonight from danger free ... *He casts a glance back: his effigy, with horns and hooves, blossoms into flame above the dock.*

Carriage. Paine stares out at his destination up ahead. Over this,

PAINE'S LETTER VOICE: ... I am become, Mr President, like the sight of water to canine madness, and for no other reason than that I have publicly denounced all other churches in claiming my **own** mind as my one and only church.

From the moving carriage we see the lit White House, newly built, surrounded by bog and wasteland.

White House. Banquet Room. Paine has his glass refilled at one end of a long mahogany table. Lifts glass.

PAINE: Your health, sir.

Close shot of President Jefferson, far end of table, smiling gently.

JEFFERSON: ... Ye will keep writing these damned incendiary works o' yours, Tom. Once it was just Kings and Tyrannies, now it's churches and priestcraft and religions ye set a torch to, is nothing sacred ...?

PAINE: My books make a bonfire of bad ideas and old lies mebbe, they never burned a human being.

Silence. Jefferson sips. Paine takes a pinch of snuff.

JEFFERSON: Ye came back alone?

PAINE: Aye.

JEFFERSON: Willie Short mentioned ye had some sort of a ...

PAINE: No.

Jefferson nods. Paine sips his wine.

JEFFERSON: And funds? D'ye have enough to live by ...?

PAINE: Much as I ever had, I guess. A man's real wealth's the people he can call friend, your invitation to come an' see ye here put a smile on an old man's face, I tell ye, mister ...

JEFFERSON: I did no more than I felt, Tom.

PAINE: Ye've enough in your dish without takin' risks on my account ...

JEFFERSON: Tom ...

A knock at the door. Jefferson turns to look. A woman, handsome, black, moves confidently into the room.

JEFFERSON: Yes, I know, I know, my grandchildren want their story ...

WOMAN: I offered, they wouldn't hear of it ...

JEFFERSON: *(Taking her hand)* My good friend Sally Hemmings. Thomas Paine.

Paine's on his feet; nods his How do. The woman walks towards him, shakes his hand.

SALLY HEMMINGS: An honour, sir. I read aloud the whole of *Common Sense* to Mr Jefferson there - he had a migraine, I believe - back in Virginia, when we wus just all settin' out. Welcome home, Mr Paine.

PAINE: Thank ye, ma'am. Glad to meet ye.

JEFFERSON: Tell 'em I'm on my way, eh ...? *(She smiles; begins to leave)* Join us later, if ye're free. *(She nods; leaves. His eyes follow her all the way)* Tom. I choose the risks I take, all right? And while I'm this side of it, that door is always open. *(He stands; drains his glass)* A few minutes, unh? Family matters ...

He leaves. Paine stands. Stretches. Walks a long wall of portraits: Sam Adams, John Adams, John Jay, John Hancock, Gouverneur Morris, George Washington, Thomas Jefferson, Ben Franklin.

Paine's face, staring up.

Long shot of the room: it's as before, but Paine is missing; erased from the record.

Philadelphia. *Coach station by docks. Evening. Paine debarks from the Washington coach, slings satchel over shoulder. An African driver leaves his open shallop, approaches him.*

DRIVER: Mista Paine, is it, sir? *(Paine nods, surprised)* This way, if ye please ...

Paine follows him to the shallop.

DRIVER: *(the satchel)* Let me carry that ...

PAINE: It's fine.

DRIVER: O.K.

Paine looks at the man; smiles to himself; boards the shallop.

Floating images from moving shallop of Paine's Philadelphia: landing quays, Ma Downey's, the London Coffee House, Aitken's bookstore, the State House; Marthe's house on Walnut. David Rittenhouse's corner cottage looms.

PAINE: What, has he moved ...?

DRIVER: Says he'll see ye Carpenters Hall, sir.

Carpenters' Hall. *Backyard. Paine stands by the shallop, scanning the deserted building for signs of life.*

MAN'S VOICE: Common Sense, as I live 'n' breathe.

Paine turns, grins; David Rittenhouse, grey, upright, stands in a doorway, shrugging on his jacket. Paine approaches. A handshake.

PAINE: Mr Rittenhouse.

RITTENHOUSE: Mr Paine.

They embrace: long, felt moment.

RITTENHOUSE: Hear they gave ye a bad time up there, when ye landed.

PAINE: I've had worse. What's happening?

RITTENHOUSE: I'm putting something right inside ... Want to join me?

PAINE: Surely. I'm free.

Carpenters' Hall, backstage. Rittenhouse's lamp guides Paine through the gloom towards the small curtained stage.

PAINE: *(arriving mid-stage)* Hold the holly there, will ye. Eyes aren't what they were ...

RITTENHOUSE: *(calling to someone above them)* Ye got any more light for Mr Paine there, boys?

Slung oil lamps begin to blossom above him. Paine stares up, dazzled. The curtains slowly part on the darkened, silent hall. Lights bloom slowly, everywhere. Six hundred working men pack the place end to end.

MATLACK: *(a voice, but unmistakable)* Welcome home, Mr Paine ...

Applause, respectful, felt, swells across the space. Matlack's face gleams up at him; Cannon's, Joseph's ... Men ripple to their feet, the disciplined din builds.

Paine looks across at Rittenhouse, who's applauding with the rest; shakes his head, face greasing with feeling.

From the back of the hall a lone tin whistle strikes up "The World Turned Upside Down". Men's voices begin to join in, the singing swells to fill the hall.

Sound fades on close shot of Paine's face, dealing with it all.

Fade in:

CARNET'S LETTER VOICE: Dearest man, Tell me you are the greatest philosopher of the age, I will not argue, but do not tell me what I may or may not do with my life. America is my destination; I **will** see you in the Spring, as promised.

New Rochelle, Farmhouse. Paine stands before the scullery mirror, struggling to put order in his unruly hair.He arrives at the main room table, gathers the much-read letter, scans it again. He wears spruce best clothes, clean shoes: still a mess.

Checks his watch. Heads for the verandah. Stares out at the thin deserted lane to the high road.

CARNET'S LETTER VOICE: If it is your wish not to be with me, then I must hear it from your own lips ...

He reaches for his stick; rejects it, heads off.

Lane. Staging post; two travellers wait for the coach to show. Paine stands at his fence, waiting too. The coach lifts suddenly over a rise, draws up at the post. The driver gets down to board the two who wait. No one gets off.

Paine's face. He turns away. Stifflegs back towards the farm, a quarter mile away, body stooped a little now, eyes down.

He walks down the dirt lane. Sounds reach him from somewhere, perhaps in his head, kids' voices calling. He turns to scan the lane behind him: it's empty. He mops his face. Turns again to the farmhouse. Sees a horse and trap outside the front door, piled with luggage. Benjamin appears on the verandah, Thomas behind him, arguing in French over who carries what. Thomas sees Paine, whoops, runs out to meet him, Benjamin in his wake. Hugs, kisses, chatter, French and English, as they lead him in.

Paine stands in the doorway, watching Carnet, sleeves up, attacking the pig sty. She hasn't seen him.

PAINE: Ye came three thousand miles to clean a house, is it?

She wrists hair from her eyes to look at him.

PAINE: Did I not tell you to wait?

CARNET: I wait for no man. Not even Paine.

188

The boys bundle past him with luggage. Carnet stands, directs them upstairs,they clatter off.

CARNET: So. This is America.

PAINE: Aye.

He turns away, walks out onto the verandah, Carnet joins him. They stare out at the empty flatlands for a moment.

PAINE: How's de Bonneville?

CARNET: He's well. Sends love.

PAINE: Any more babies?

CARNET: Uhunh.

PAINE: Ye wanta waste your life out here, I guess that's what ye'll do.

She chuckles. Slips an arm about his waist. He puts a slow, careful arm about her shoulder.

PAINE: Ain't Paris exactly though, unh?

CARNET: It'll do.

Bedroom. *Night. They lie naked under sheets, staring at each other in the narrow ancient bed. His eyes are fierce.*

CARNET: What?

PAINE: You're mad. There's not money enough to keep me, let alone you people ...

CARNET: What d'ye mean? You're flat? Ye sold two million books and not a penny left?

PAINE: Never wrote for money, never took none hardly, put it back where it came from. Writing's writing.

CARNET: Keep yourself. I'll get a job. I'll teach French.

PAINE: Out here there's just cows, they don't need it ...

CARNET: I'll go to New York.

He sniffs. Turns onto his back. Silence.

189

PAINE: *(Eventually)* Will I go with ye?

She leans across, strokes the line of his throat with a finger. He goes to speak, her finger stills his lips.

CARNET: Tais-toi. Tu es bête.

She moves again. Her face hovers above his.

CARNET: *(A whisper)* Let me love you.

A slow kiss, gentle, binding.

PAINE: Ye know, maybe there's one more book in me ...

She kisses him again, strong, more urgent.

CARNET: What'll ye call it, d'ye know? *(He shakes his head)* The future. *(His eyes search the meaning)* Call it The Future.

New Rochelle Farm; barn. *Humid air; thunder, close; light fading. Benjamin puts horse and trap together.*

Farmhouse, main room. Paine struggles into his overcoat, ready for out. He stands by the table, helping Thomas with geometry. Carnet appears on the stair, manuscript in hand, talking as she comes.

CARNET: ... There's a part I don't follow in this piece ...

She sees him, stops. He looks up at her, buttoning his coat.

CARNET: This is no weather for taking a walk, Paine ...

PAINE: Ain't taking a walk, love. Benjamin's fetchin' the trap round. Gonna cast my vote.

CARNET: Ye'll be soaked ... leave it, man.

PAINE: *(Factual)* Lotta people died makin' it possible, makes a right a duty ...

Benjamin bangs in.

BENJAMIN: All yours, Paine.

PAINE: Thank ye. *(To both)* Wanna see your geometry on that table when I get back, ok? *(To Carnet)* I'll be an hour.

CARNET: *(As he leaves)* At least take your damn stick.

PAINE: *(Over shoulder)* Can't. Threw it away.

Polling Station. *New Rochelle. The rain-rattled rudimentary church hall all but deserted. The Returning Officer holds his watch in his hand, waiting to close and seal the boxes. Several helpers drink tea down the room. Turn to stare as Paine walks in from the night, rain streaming from his sodden frame. The Returning Officer watches his approach up the hall, distaste in his eyes.*

OFFICER: Paine, isn't it?

PAINE: It is.

OFFICER: I'm afraid you're not qualified to vote here, sir.

PAINE: I have the farm at Hob's End ...

OFFICER: So I understand.

PAINE: Don't that qualify me?

OFFICER: 'Fraid not. Not if y'ain't American, it don't.

Long pause, as Paine absorbs it. Puddles have formed at his feet. His white hair's plastered to his skull.

PAINE: You sayin' I ain't American?

OFFICER: Exactly so.

Paine nods. A bright terrible anger works its way through him, leaks into the eyes.

PAINE: I may just have to sue the shit outa you, mister ...

OFFICER: And I may just have to get the law round here if ye insist on usin' that kinda language on church premises, we don't swear in God's presence in these parts. Ye've no vote here, sir. That's it.

Paine half turns, as if to leave, then surges forward, empowered by rage, upends the table against the officer's chest, dumping him on his arse against the wall. The guy almost passes out with shock, the men down the room

191

have frozen where they stand. Paine sucks air for a moment, coming to.

PAINE: You know the problem wi' pisspots like you, mister? Ye actually believe God is on your side ...

He turns. Walks stiffly out.

Farmhouse. *The rain has eased. Carnet sits at a desk by the bedroom window, trying to work, attention fixed on outside. Her nib buckles on the page, she searches drawers for a replacement, lifts out some documents, discovers Paine's Will. Gazes at it blankly, fear showing in her eyes. Sound of trap outside the house.*

Paine stands in the doorway, sodden, still. She reaches the main room, a towel in her hand, closes the door behind him, he stands in silence, shadowed, as she removes his coat.

CARNET: Strip by the fire, I'll dry ye ...

Sounds outside. The horse whinneys.

PAINE: *(Numb)* Gotta put the horse under ...

CARNET: Come, I'll do it ...

She walks him carefully to the fireside. Begins to unbutton his shirt. Laboriously helps it from his back.

CARNET: Take them off. I'll fetch another cloth ...

His hands move to his belt. She leaves for the kitchen. Hears a thud behind her. Screams.

Cut to

Bedroom. *Day. Paine lies, face waxen, eyes closed, in the narrow bed. His hair's been trimmed, tidied; he wears a gleaming white nightshirt. Sun streams across him from the little window.*

Sounds of voices from outside on the verandah. The eyes blink open, screw a little to listen. Good-days, a horse canters off. Carnet's feet on the stair. She enters quietly, a red rose in a vase in her hand.

PAINE: S'that the doctor?

CARNET: Aye.

PAINE: Did he come up?

CARNET: Briefly.

PAINE: Did he take my legs with him? *(She smiles)* Someone did. *(She busies herself; sets the rose by his bed)* Speak to the Quakers? *(She nods)* Won't have me, eh? *(She shakes her head)* The big field'll do as well.

CARNET: There's a minister come, wants to pray for your soul ...

PAINE: Tell 'im t'bugger off.

She sits at his side on the bed. Teases strands of hair from his brow.

CARNET: Paine ...

PAINE: Call me Tom. Just once. Want to hear it.

CARNET: Tom. Aye.

PAINE: S'he still down there, the minister? *(She nods)* Will we give him a song?

She smiles. Helps a second pillow under his head, to lift him. Lays an arm about his shoulder.

Paine begins to sing: The World Turned Upside Down. After a while she joins him. Thomas and Benjamin appear on the stair-landing; watch them through the open door.

MIX SLOWLY THROUGH TO

Fields. *Day. June, 1809. A small trail of carts and carriages heads across fields.*

Big field. A coffin lowered into a simple grave; a headstone nearby:

Thomas Paine, age 73, author of Common Sense.

A handful of people gathered at graveside. Two black men, father and son, stand respectfully by, their trousers spattered from their journey. Carnet motions her sons to the grave-head, stations herself at its foot.

CARNET: *(Red rose held against black dress)* May the body of this man lie in peace in this good earth. And may his name be remembered wherever Liberty and Justice are cherished ... *(Looks down the grave at son Thomas)* Let my son there stand here for America ... I for France.

BLACK FATHER: Amen.

Carnet turns, smiles at him. The man steps forward, hat in hand. Collects a hunk of dirt.

BLACK FATHER: I hope ye'll forgive th'intrusion, ma'am. My son 'n' me heered Mr Paine'd passed on, we walk' up from New York t'pay respec's ...

CARNET: You're very welcome, gentlemen.

He throws the dirt on the coffin. His son joins him.

Wide, high shot of the scene. The two black men peel away, the diggers head for their tool-cart, the boys leave their mother to a private moment.

She stands some moments longer, turns away, clears frame. For a moment, there is only the open grave.

The shot closes in, begins to move, as Paine's voice sets up, over, in a final summation of belief, as if from the grave.

PAINE'S VOICE: ... The present state of civilization is as odious at it is unjust ...

The down-shot heads on past the grave, slowly covers the fields and hedges beyond.

PAINE'S VOICE: ... It is absolutely the opposite of what it should be, and it is necessary that a revolution should be made in it ...

The down-shot heads on: odd sounds approaching traffic on a highway.

PAINE'S VOICE: ... The contrast of affluence and
  wretchedness, continually meeting and offending the
  eye, is like dead and living bodies chained together ...

*The shot tilts suddenly, reveals a modern highway, heavy
with traffic, ripping past New Rochelle. Mixes, with the
southbound flow, to today's New York City and its images
of wretchedness and affluence ...*

PAINE'S VOICE: ... The great mass of the poor are become
  an hereditary race, and it is next to impossible for them
  to get out of that state of themselves ... The condition
  of millions in every country ... is now far worse than if
  they had been born before civilisation began ...

*The shot resolves slowly back to the deserted field, the
open grave.*

PAINE'S VOICE: ... It is a revolution in the state of
  civilization that is now needed. Already the conviction
  that representation is the true system of government is
  spreading itself fast in the world. But there must grow,
  and soon, a system of civilization out of that system of
  government, so organized that not a man or woman
  born in the Republic but shall inherit some means of
  beginning the world and see before them the certainty
  of escaping the miseries that up to now have always
  accompanied old age ... An army of principle will
  penetrate where an army of soldiers can not: it will
  march on the horizon of the world, and it will conquer.

A wind stirs the grass: the grave remains open.

- End -

Sons
and
Lovers

Trevor Griffiths'
screenplay of the novel by
D.H.Lawrence

The screenplay of Trevor Griffiths' celebrated television version of Sons and Lovers provides a striking new perspective on the classic novel.

Griffiths never enters into a commission lightly, and this script will repay careful study, both as a masterly piece of dramatic writing and as an unusually incisive reading of Lawrence's original. It is clear that in Griffiths, English letters has acquired a major and glittering talent.

320 pages, illustrated paperback,
ISBN 0 85124 334 7 £7.95

Available from Spokesman Books
www.spokesmanbooks.com

Sons and Lovers

Trevor Griffiths'
screenplay of the novel by
D.H.Lawrence

The scripts of Trevor Griffithsí celebrated
television version of Sons and Lovers provides a
striking new perspective on the classic novel.

Griffiths never enters into a commission lightly,
and this script will repay careful study, both as a
masterly piece of dramatic writing and as an
unusually incisive reading of Lawrenceís original.
It is clear that in Griffiths, English letters has
acquired a major and glittering talent.

320 pages, illustrated paperback,
ISBN 0 85124 334 7 £7.95

Sons
and
Lover

Trevor Griffiths'
screenplay of the novel by
D.H.Lawrence

The scripts of Trevor Griffiths' celebrated
television version of Sons and Lovers
provides a striking new perspective on the
classic novel.

Griffiths never enters into a commission
lightly, and this script will repay careful
study, both as a masterly piece of dramatic
writing and as an unusually incisive reading
of Lawrence's original. It is clear that in
Griffiths, English letters has acquired a
major and glittering talent.

320 pages, illustrated paperback,
ISBN 0 85124 334 7 £7.95